The Great International Dessert Cookbook

The Great International Dessert Cookbook

80 Easy and Elegant Recipes—
a Glorious Celebration
of Global Delights

HONEY & LARRY ZISMAN
with the help and cooperation of
the U. S. Committee for UNICEF

ST. MARTIN'S PRESS □ New York

The designations employed and the presentation of the
material in these pages do not imply the expression of
any opinion whatsoever on the part of the Secretariat of
the United Nations or of UNICEF.

THE GREAT INTERNATIONAL DESSERT COOKBOOK. Copyright ©
1985 by Honey and Larry Zisman. All rights reserved.
Printed in the United States of America. No part of this
book may be used or reproduced in any manner
whatsoever without written permission except in the
case of brief quotations embodied in critical articles or
reviews. For information, address St. Martin's Press, 175
Fifth Avenue, New York, N.Y. 10010.

Design by Janet Tingey

Library of Congress Cataloging in Publication Data
Zisman, Honey.
   The great international dessert cookbook.
   1. Desserts I. Zisman, Larry. II. Title.
TX773.Z57 1985   641.8′6   85-12505
ISBN 0-312-34596-8 (pbk.)

Cover: LA RONDE DU MONDE, contributed by Ljubir Milinkov
(Yugoslavia/United States of America). UNICEF card forthcoming.

First Edition
10 9 8 7 6 5 4 3 2 1

for Boris and Esther
who have already traveled the world

Our sincere thanks to
the diplomats from all around the world who so generously shared
with us their best dessert recipes

CONTENTS

INTRODUCTION

UNICEF: The United Nations Children's Fund

The U.S. Committee for UNICEF is proud to be cooperating with Honey and Larry Zisman on *The Great International Dessert Cookbook*. Our involvement in this book gives us the opportunity to help reach you, the reader, with an important message: that the needs of the world's children could be met, if only the necessary will, and some very modest means, were to be made available.

UNICEF—the United Nations Children's Fund—is working with governments in 115 developing countries to help bring about a virtual revolution in child survival techniques. By implementing four simple measures—mass immunization against childhood diseases, breast-feeding instead of bottle-feeding, oral rehydration for severely dehydrated children, and growth monitoring—the lives of up to 20,000 children could be saved each day.

The U.S. Committee for UNICEF was formed to raise funds for UNICEF-assisted programs overseas and to increase American awareness of the needs of children. It is the largest volunteer-supported endeavor in the United States with over 3,000,000 adults and children participating. Each year, the president of the United States officially proclaims October 31st—Halloween—as National UNICEF Day and thousands of children "trick or treat" for UNICEF across the country. Through the sales of greeting cards, stationery, books, and educational materials, the Committee raises additional funds.

The reproduction of some of UNICEF's past greeting card designs to brighten the pages of this book offers a rich and rewarding taste of UNICEF's world-famous greeting card program. As with UNICEF cards, gifts, and stationery, proceeds to UNICEF from the sale of this book help provide vaccines, clean water, education, and adequate nutrition for children in need.

The U.S. Committee for UNICEF would like to express its appreciation to the Zismans for contributing a portion of their earnings from this book to help the world's children. We hope that the broad appeal of the book and UNICEF's work will help link the world through a commitment to children.

Delicious Desserts from around the World

When Jules Verne sent Phileas Fogg on his journey in *Around the World in 80 Days*, Mr. Fogg won a wager of twenty thousand pounds sterling and married Aouda, the beautiful Indian princess.

Your voyage around the world in *The Great International Dessert Cookbook* will gain treasures for you, too, although somewhat different from those won by Mr. Fogg. You will have the pleasures of eating and serving exquisite desserts that will surely delight you, your family, and your guests.

Sweet treats for dessert are popular throughout the world and we have collected exclusively for this book eighty of the best dessert recipes from eighty different countries on six continents.

You will find here coffee cream puffs from Brazil, brandied oranges from the Sudan, Norwegian cherry almond cake, Australian meringue and fruit torte, and seventy-six other delightful, authentic desserts from around the world.

These recipes are easy to make, use readily available ingredients, and, most important, taste deliciously different from just about anything else you have ever had before.

So start your adventure, your own voyage of delicious discovery, and just like Phileas Fogg you, too, will be rewarded with memorable and enduring treasures.

NORTH AMERICA

CANADA

1 cup maple sugar
½ cup lightly packed brown sugar
1 cup butter or margarine
2 cups soft wheat (pastry) flour
1 teaspoon baking powder
1 egg
1 tablespoon water

Maple Sugar Cookies

The maple leaf is the national symbol of Canada—there is one in the center of the Canadian flag—and there is no better good-will ambassador for that country than these delicious maple sugar cookies.

1. Preheat oven to 350° F.
2. Cream together sugars and butter. Sift together flour and baking powder and add to sugars. Blend in egg and water.
3. Roll out dough on a floured surface to ⅛-inch thickness. Cut with floured cookie cutters of different designs and place 1 inch apart on a lightly greased cookie sheet.
4. Bake at 350° F for 5 to 8 minutes, until golden brown.

Yield: approximately 6 dozen cookies

CANADA □ The parks in Canada's capital city of Ottawa blossom each spring with a special display of flowers, thanks to the people of the Netherlands.

Canada provided refuge to the exiled royal family of Holland during World War II, and in a continuing show of gratitude the Dutch government each year sends to Ottawa three million tulips, six hundred thousand daffodils, and half a million crocuses for planting throughout the city.

2

MEXICO

½ cup butter or margarine, softened
2 cups packed brown sugar
2 eggs
1 teaspoon vanilla extract
6 ounces unsweetened chocolate,
   grated
2 cups flour
1 teaspoon baking soda
1¼ cups milk
Creamy Chocolate Frosting (recipe
   follows)

Brown Sugar Chocolate Cake

Chocolate and vanilla are popular flavorings in many Mexican desserts and this chocolate cake is a good example of the combination of those two flavors.

1. Preheat oven to 350° F.
2. In a large mixing bowl, beat butter until light. Gradually add brown sugar, mixing together well. Add eggs, one at a time, beating well after each addition. Stir in vanilla and grated chocolate. Set aside.
3. Combine flour and baking soda. Add flour mixture, alternately with milk, to butter mixture, and beat until smooth.
4. Pour batter into a greased and floured 9x13-inch baking pan and bake at 350° F for 35 to 40 minutes, until cake tests clean.
5. Let cool completely on a wire rack. Remove from pan and frost with Creamy Chocolate Frosting.
   Yield: 10 to 12 servings

(continued)

CREAMY CHOCOLATE FROSTING

6 ounces unsweetened chocolate
2 cups confectioners' sugar
¼ cup boiling water
Dash salt
2 eggs
¼ cup butter or margarine, softened
1 teaspoon vanilla extract

Melt chocolate over hot water. Remove from heat and stir in sugar, boiling water, and salt. Add eggs and beat until smooth. Add butter and vanilla, mixing well.

MEXICO □ Baja California is the long thin peninsula in northwestern Mexico that extends southward from California between the Pacific Ocean and the Gulf of California. It is so different from the rest of the country that Mexicans refer to it as *el otro mundo*, another world.

Although there are numerous roads, hotels, resorts, restaurants, and other facilities catering to travelers, with more being built each year, Baja California is still very much a wilderness area. Some people say it is one of the last frontiers in North America.

It is the ideal place for someone wishing to find solitude on uninhabited sparkling beaches, view the stars with no interference from city lights, admire truly unspoiled natural scenery, study primitive rock paintings left by Indians ten thousand years ago, or just get away from telephones, television, daily mail deliveries, and all the other benefits of modern living.

UNITED STATES

1 cup sugar
¼ cup flour
½ teaspoon ground cinnamon
⅛ teaspoon ground nutmeg
Dash salt
8 cups peeled apple slices
1 tablespoon lemon juice
2 tablespoons butter or margarine
Pie Crust (recipe follows)
Vanilla ice cream

PIE CRUST
1½ cups flour
¼ teaspoon salt
½ teaspoon baking powder
¼ cup water
½ cup shortening, melted

Deep-Dish Apple Pie

What could be more American than the flag, motherhood, baseball, the Fourth of July, and this old-fashioned deep-dish apple pie?

1. Preheat oven to 425° F.
2. Combine sugar, flour, cinnamon, nutmeg, and salt, mixing together well. Put into a 9-inch square baking dish. Add apple slices, sprinkle lemon juice over top, and mix well. Dot with butter.
3. Cover with Pie Crust and cut several slits in top of crust.
4. Bake at 425° F for about 50 minutes, until crust is browned.
5. Serve warm topped with vanilla ice cream.
Yield: 6 to 8 servings

1. Combine flour, salt, baking powder, water, and shortening, mixing until dough becomes smooth.
2. Roll out dough on a floured surface into a 9-inch square.

UNITED STATES □ One of the largest statues in the world is officially named Liberty Enlightening the World, but to people everywhere it is much better known as the Statue of Liberty. Inscribed on a tablet attached to the base of the statue is Emma Lazarus's famous poem

"The New Colossus," which ends with the inspiring line, "I lift my lamp beside the golden door."

Indeed, the torch of the Statue of Liberty stood high over New York Harbor for nearly one hundred years, welcoming millions of new arrivals to the United States.

A massive restoration of the Statue of Liberty was started in 1983 and included the replacement of the torch with a new one.

The original torch can now be seen by visitors—up close, rather than three hundred feet above them—in an exhibit on Liberty Island at the base of the statue.

CENTRAL AMERICA

EL SALVADOR

3 cups flour
4 teaspoons baking powder
4 cups water
½ cup plus 2 tablespoons butter or
*   margarine*
½ teaspoon salt
10 eggs
Vegetable shortening (enough to fill
*   frying utensil to 3 inches)*
Dark corn syrup

Fried Dough Puffs

These dough puffs are not exactly doughnuts, they are not cakes, and you cannot call them cookies. They are just what their name says—fried dough puffs—and they are, to say the least, quite tasty.

1. Sift together flour and baking powder. Set aside.
2. Combine water, butter, and salt in a heavy saucepan and cook over medium heat, stirring constantly, until butter melts and mixture comes to a rolling boil. Stir in sifted flour.
3. Remove from heat. Add eggs, one at a time, mixing well after each addition.
4. Heat vegetable shortening to very hot and drop dough by teaspoonfuls, two or three at a time, into shortening. Fry until dough puffs up. Remove and drain on paper towels.
5. Serve hot or cold with dark corn syrup.
Yield: approximately 3 dozen puffs

EL SALVADOR □ The Pipil Indians of El Salvador called their country Cuscutlán, the "Land of Precious Things." They were truthfully describing the natural beauties of the land in which they lived.

The Pipil list of El Salvador's precious things included colorful exotic wild birds; orchids, jasmine, lavenders, and other tropical flowers;

bougainvillea vines with brilliantly colored leaves; waterfalls; mangrove swamps; lakes of deep blue water in extinct volcano craters; magnificent mountaintop vistas; pine forests; bubbling hot mineral springs; and unspoiled Pacific beaches shaded by palm trees.

GUATEMALA

2 cups mashed very ripe bananas
1½ tablespoons lemon juice
½ cup sugar
½ teaspoon salt
2 eggs, beaten
1 cup milk
1½ teaspoons vanilla extract
1 pint heavy or light cream

Banana Ice Cream

Making your own ice cream at home cannot be any easier than this banana treat.

1. Mix together bananas, lemon juice, and sugar. Add salt, eggs, milk, and vanilla, mixing together well. Stir in cream.
2. Spoon mixture into a 2-quart container, smooth out top, and freeze.

Yield: approximately 2 quarts ice cream

GUATEMALA □ The Mayan ceremonial center at Tikal, in the jungles of El Petén Province in north-central Guatemala, is one of the most important sites of its kind. Tikal was used by the Mayas from about 200 B.C. until A.D. 900, when it was abandoned for reasons that are still not known.

More than three thousand buildings have been found, as well as thousands of monuments, art objects, and religious altars. The focal

9

point of Tikal is the Great Plaza and an area of about six square miles around it has already been excavated. It is believed, however, that the entire Mayan community at Tikal was spread over an area four times larger than that which has already been uncovered.

HONDURAS

2 eggs, beaten
½ cup red wine
6 slices French bread, each about
   ¾-inch thick
2 tablespoons butter or margarine
½ cup raisins
¼ cup honey
¼ teaspoon ground cloves
Confectioners' sugar

Honey Wine Toast

There are similarities between honey wine toast and the usual French toast: both are slices of bread soaked in eggs and then fried. But it is like comparing a Mercedes-Benz and a Volkswagen because they both have wheels and go on the highway. When you serve this dessert at a dinner party, everyone will ask for the recipe so they can serve it themselves the next time they entertain.

1. Combine eggs and ¼ cup of the wine. Soak bread slices in mixture.
2. Melt butter in a large pan over medium heat and fry bread slices on both sides until golden brown. Remove from pan and set aside.
3. Mix together remaining ¼ cup wine, raisins, honey, and cloves in the same pan. Return bread slices to pan, cover, and cook for about 15 minutes over low heat.

10

4. Remove bread slices, spoon wine sauce from pan over bread, and sprinkle with confectioners' sugar.
Yield: 6 servings

HONDURAS □ Christopher Columbus, who landed in Honduras in 1502, gave that country its name—the Spanish word for "depths"—because of the deep waters off its northern coast.

PANAMA

3 cups flaked coconut
1 cup sweetened condensed milk
1 cup water
1 cup sugar
¼ teaspoon vanilla extract
Cherries

Coconut Candy Balls

Panama is best known for the Canal that connects the Atlantic and Pacific oceans but as more people learn about these chewy coconut candies, the country will get another national symbol.

1. Combine coconut, milk, water, and sugar in a heavy saucepan and cook over medium heat, stirring constantly, for about 35 minutes, until mixture thickens. Mix in vanilla. Remove from heat and let cool completely.
2. Using dampened hands, shape mixture into 1-inch balls and place into candy papers.

3. Cut cherries into large pieces and decorate top of candy balls. Store in refrigerator.

Yield: approximately 6 dozen candies

PANAMA □ Passengers on ships that travel through the Panama Canal get spectacular views of unspoiled natural scenery as well as the chance to see up close the operations of one of the great modern engineering achievements. The Canal uses as much water in one day—raising and lowering ships as they pass from one ocean to the other—as the city of Boston does in two weeks.

Because of a twist in the geography of Panama, the Pacific Ocean entrance to the Canal is farther to the east than is the entrance at the Atlantic Ocean end.

THE CARIBBEAN

ANTIGUA AND BARBUDA

2 eggs, beaten
2 teaspoons sugar
¼ teaspoon grated lime peel
1 teaspoon vanilla extract
1 cup hot milk
1½ cups flaked coconut
Pie Crust (recipe follows)

PIE CRUST
1 cup flour
Dash salt
4 tablespoons butter or margarine,
    softened
4 tablespoons shortening
2 tablespoons ice water

Coconut Custard Pie

Hundreds of products are made from the coconut palm tree—from soap to cooking oil, from brooms to candy—but not one of them is as tasty as this coconut custard pie from the Caribbean.

1. Preheat oven to 400° F.
2. Beat together eggs, sugar, and lime peel. Add vanilla, milk, and coconut, stirring well.
3. Pour filling into unbaked Pie Crust and bake at 400° F for about 25 minutes, until set.
4. Let cool and then chill in refrigerator. Serve cold.
Yield: 6 to 8 servings

1. Sift flour and salt together. Add butter and shortening, working with fingers until mixture becomes crumbly. Slowly mix in ice water.
2. Shape dough into a ball, wrap tightly in wax paper, and place on ice cubes for about 15 minutes.
3. Dip hands into ice water and press dough into a 9-inch pie plate.

ANTIGUA AND BARBUDA □ The attractive island scenery and the even, mild climate of the Leeward Islands at the eastern edge of the Caribbean Sea—average summer temperature: 84 degrees F; average winter

14

temperature: 75 degrees F—attract many visitors to Antigua and Barbuda.

Tourism has become such a dominant part of the country's economy that nearly 60 percent of the labor force works in the tourist industry.

BAHAMAS

¼ cup butter or margarine, softened
1 cup sugar
3 eggs, beaten
2 cups guava paste
½ teaspoon ground nutmeg
½ teaspoon ground cinnamon
¼ teaspoon ground cloves
3 cups flour
2 teaspoons baking powder
Hard Sauce (recipe follows)

Guava Mold

The advertising campaign to attract tourists to the Bahamas uses the slogan "It's better in the Bahamas." One of the many things that are better in the Bahamas is this thick pudding with the flavor of rum and the guava fruit.

1. Cream butter with sugar. Add eggs, guava paste, nutmeg, cinnamon, and cloves, working in with fingers until mixture is smooth. Sift together flour and baking powder and add to mixture, working in well. Batter will be stiff.
2. Spoon batter evenly into a greased 3-quart ovenware dish, smooth out top, and cover.
3. Place dish in a large pan and pour in boiling water to come one third the way up the sides of the ovenware dish.

15

4. Cook pudding in the boiling water for 3 hours, adding water to the pan as needed to maintain the original level.

5. Let cool slightly, remove from mold, and serve with Hard Sauce.
Yield: 6 to 8 servings

HARD SAUCE
½ cup butter or margarine, softened
1 cup confectioners' sugar
2 tablespoons rum

Cream butter with sugar, gradually adding rum. Chill in refrigerator.

BAHAMAS □ The tourist industry in the Bahamas owes its beginnings to a royal scandal that shocked England during the 1930s and to the onset of World War II.

In December 1936, King Edward VIII abdicated the throne of England in order to marry American divorcée Wallis Warfield Simpson. The following year, with their new titles of the Duke and Duchess of Windsor, the newlyweds left England in self-imposed exile. During a visit to England in 1939, the Duke volunteered to assist in the war effort, so his brother, King George VI, appointed the Duke governor of the Bahama Islands, at that time a British colony.

The Duke and Duchess attracted many of their rich and socially prominent friends to the Bahamas during the 1940s and 1950s. The publicity the islands received from these visitors, combined with the development of fast and inexpensive jet travel and the growth of the cruise ship business out of Florida, has made the Bahamas today a major destination for tourists seeking warmth, sun, sand, ocean, gambling, and the carefree vacation that an island resort offers.

BARBADOS

6 medium yams
1 cup crushed pineapple
1 tablespoon lemon juice
¼ cup butter or margarine, melted
½ cup brown sugar
½ cup granulated sugar
1 teaspoon grated lemon peel
½ teaspoon salt
½ teaspoon ground nutmeg
Chopped nuts
Flaked coconut

Yam and Pineapple Delight

This yam and pineapple dish is served as a dessert in Barbados, but it also makes a very nice side dish for the main course.

1. Bake yams at 375° F for about 1 or 1½ hours, until tender. Remove from oven.
2. Lower oven heat to 350° F.
3. Take off skins from yams, slice, and place slices in a 2½-quart ovenware dish. Spoon pineapple over top. Sprinkle lemon juice and butter over pineapple. Combine sugars, lemon peel, salt, and nutmeg and sprinkle evenly over top. Cover with lid.
4. Bake at 350° F for 30 minutes. Remove cover and bake for another 30 minutes.
5. Sprinkle with chopped nuts and coconut.
Yield: 6 to 8 servings

BARBADOS □ The boast made by so many cities and towns of colonial America that "George Washington slept here" can also be made by Bridgetown, the capital of Barbados.

Washington's brother Lawrence became seriously ill in 1751 and decided to go to Barbados because the warm climate there would be

17

good for his health. Lawrence asked George to accompany him and George agreed, making the only foreign trip in his life.

While in Barbados with his brother, Washington compared the farming methods on the Caribbean island with those in Virginia.

Washington rented a house for himself on Upper Bay Street in Bridgetown for fifteen pounds sterling a month, not including liquor or laundry. That house is still standing and can be visited today.

HAITI

¼ cup butter or margarine, melted
4 tablespoons flour
1½ cups light cream, scalded
3 tablespoons grated orange peel
2 teaspoons orange extract
2 tablespoons brandy
5 egg yolks
5 tablespoons granulated sugar
1 orange
2 tablespoons confectioners' sugar
6 egg whites, stiffly beaten

Orange Soufflé

The warm pleasant weather of this Caribbean island is well reflected in this gorgeous-looking, light and airy orange treat.

1. Combine butter and flour in a heavy pan, mixing together until smooth. Gradually add cream and cook over medium heat, stirring constantly, until mixture begins to boil. Reduce heat to low and cook for 5 minutes more, stirring occasionally. Add orange peel, orange extract, and brandy.

2. Remove from heat and set aside to cool for 10 minutes.

3. Beat together egg yolks and granulated sugar in a large bowl. Gradually add cream mixture, beating constantly to prevent curdling. Set aside to cool for 20 minutes more.

4. Preheat oven to 350° F.

5. Peel orange and cut into thin slices. Place orange slices in the bottom of a 2-quart soufflé or ovenware dish that has been greased and dusted with confectioners' sugar. Sprinkle orange slices with confectioners' sugar.

6. Gently fold egg whites into cream mixture and pour into soufflé dish.

7. Bake at 350° F for 30 to 40 minutes, until lightly browned and well set in center. Do not open the oven door for at least the first 20 minutes of baking. Remove from oven and serve immediately to prevent soufflé from falling.

Yield: 4 servings

HAITI □ The Iron Market in Port-au-Prince, the capital of Haiti, is a huge and very busy bazaar housing an amazing variety of goods for sale, including native paintings, hand-carved mahogany, antiques, clothing, and a great selection of local foods.

In spite of the crowds of people and the attraction of soon-to-be-discovered bargains, first-time visitors to the market cannot help but stop and wonder what this Middle Eastern looking building with its Moslem minarets is doing on an island in the Caribbean Sea.

It seems that the designer of the Iron Market, Alexandre Gustave Eiffel—the engineer who built the famous tower in Paris—made a mistake in some shipping instructions and the Iron Market was sent to Haiti rather than to the city in Pakistan where it was originally supposed to go.

JAMAICA

1 cup sugar
5 egg yolks
5 egg whites, stiffly beaten
1 cup flour
1 tablespoon lime juice
1 teaspoon grated lime peel
Mocha Butter Frosting (recipe follows)

Mocha Layer Cake

A list of the Caribbean pleasures found on the island of Jamaica includes plenty of sun, great beaches, refreshing surf, calypso melodies, and this light and airy sponge cake with a delicious citrus flavor.

1. Preheat oven to 350° F.
2. Beat sugar into egg yolks until mixture is thick and creamy. Gently fold in egg whites. Sprinkle flour, lime juice, and lime peel over top and fold together just until flour can no longer be seen. Do not overfold.
3. Pour batter into two completely greased and floured 9-inch cake pans. Spread evenly and smooth out top.
4. Bake on middle rack of oven at 350° F for about 20 minutes, until toothpick tests clean.
5. Let cool for about 5 minutes, remove from pans, and cool completely on wire racks. Using a large serrated knife, cut each cake layer in half horizontally, making four layers.
6. Stack the four layers, spreading Mocha Butter Frosting between the layers and on the top and sides of the cake. Store in refrigerator.

Yield: 8 to 10 servings

MOCHA BUTTER FROSTING

2 cups unsalted butter or margarine,
  softened
1¼ cups sugar
2 tablespoons instant coffee powder
  dissolved in ½ cup hot water
8 egg yolks, beaten until they are
  thick and pale
2 tablespoons rum

1. Cream butter until light and fluffy. Set aside.
2. Combine sugar and dissolved coffee in a small saucepan and bring to a boil over medium heat, stirring until sugar dissolves. Continue cooking at a full boil for about 10 minutes, until syrup thickens and a small amount dropped into cold water immediately forms a soft ball.
3. Immediately pour hot syrup slowly into egg yolks, beating constantly. Continue beating for another 10 to 15 minutes, until mixture cools to room temperature and becomes thick and smooth.
4. Beat in creamed butter, a little at a time. Stir in rum.

JAMAICA □ The elegant Round Hill resort sits on a peninsula jutting out into the Caribbean Sea near Montego Bay on Jamaica's north shore. It has been a favorite gathering place of the international jet set for many years.

Guests who sit down and pick at the keyboard on the resort's piano are fingering the same keys that were played by Sir Noel Coward, Cole Porter, Irving Berlin, and Richard Rodgers when they stayed at the Round Hill.

SOUTH AMERICA

ARGENTINA

3 cups flour
2 cups sugar
1 cup shortening
1 teaspoon grated lemon peel
6 medium apples
1 cup warm milk
2 eggs
¼ cup brandy or whiskey
1 teaspoon vanilla extract
Vanilla ice cream, if desired

Apple Crumb

This apple cake tastes as good with breakfast coffee as it does after a late dinner.

1. Preheat oven to 350° F.
2. Mix together flour and sugar. Cut in shortening until mixture resembles coarse crumbs. Mix in lemon peel.
3. Place half the flour mixture in the bottom of a greased and floured 9x13-inch baking pan. Set aside.
4. Peel, core, and slice apples. Place half the apple slices on top of mixture in baking pan. Top with remaining flour mixture and then remaining apple slices. Set aside.
5. Beat together milk, eggs, brandy, and vanilla extract and pour over apples.
6. Bake at 350° F for about 1 hour, until golden brown. Cool on wire rack.
7. Serve warm with vanilla ice cream, if desired.
Yield: 10 to 12 servings

ARGENTINA □ The Iguaçu Falls in the extreme northeastern part of Argentina are a spectacular sight in the middle of a rugged forest setting.

24

The waterfalls form a semicircular arc more than two miles wide and spill over a crest 230 feet high on the Paraná River. By comparison, Niagara Falls is only 180 feet high and the combined width of the American and Canadian falls is less than half as wide as the Iguaçu.

The word Iguaçu means "The Great Water" in the language of the Guarani Indians of central South America, and in this case there is no exaggeration.

BRAZIL

1 cup butter or margarine
Dash salt
2 cups boiling water
2 cups flour
8 eggs
¼ cup cold strong coffee
1 teaspoon sugar
2 cups heavy cream, whipped, or
  frozen whipped topping, thawed
Coffee Rum Sauce (recipe follows)

Coffee Cream Puffs with Coffee Rum Sauce

Some people may think of coffee as nothing more than a drink to get them started in the morning, but these cream puffs raise coffee to an art form with a taste that is not just for breakfast anymore.

1. Preheat oven to 400° F.
2. Combine butter, salt, and water in a saucepan and cook over high heat, stirring occasionally, until butter melts. Remove from heat. Add flour and beat until mixture leaves side of pan and forms a smooth ball. Beat in eggs, one at a time.
3. Using a teaspoon, shape dough into 1-inch balls and place on a lightly greased cookie sheet.

4. Bake at 400° F for 10 minutes, reduce heat to 350° F, and bake for 15 minutes more, until light brown.

5. Let cool and slice puffs in half.

6. Fold coffee and sugar into whipped heavy cream and spoon into puffs. Arrange puffs in a tower on a serving dish and drizzle warm Coffee Rum Sauce over top and along sides of tower.

Yield: approximately 3½ dozen cream puffs

COFFEE RUM SAUCE

2 tablespoons cornstarch
3 tablespoons cold coffee
1 cup sugar
1½ cups strong coffee
2 tablespoons butter or margarine
2 tablespoons rum

1. Mix together cornstarch and cold coffee. Set aside.

2. Combine sugar and strong coffee in a saucepan and cook over low heat, stirring constantly, until sugar dissolves. Add cornstarch mixture and cook until mixture boils and becomes thick.

3. Remove from heat and add butter and rum, stirring until butter melts. Let cool slightly.

BRAZIL □ Soccer is the most popular sport in Brazil and the Maracaña Municipal Stadium in Rio de Janeiro, with a seating capacity of 205,000, is the largest soccer stadium in the world.

By comparison, the largest football stadium in the United States is the Rose Bowl in Pasadena, California, and can hold just under 107,000 fans.

CHILE

½ cup flour
Dash salt
½ cup water
¼ cup shortening
2 eggs
Cream Filling (recipe follows)
Chocolate Frosting (recipe follows)

Chocolate Éclairs

These éclairs with old-fashioned egg cream filling and rich chocolate icing will become everyone's favorite.

1. Preheat oven to 425° F.
2. Sift together flour and salt. Set aside.
3. Combine water and shortening in a saucepan and cook over medium heat until water boils. Turn heat to low and immediately add flour all at once. Beat quickly with a wooden spoon and continue until mixture leaves sides of the pan and forms a stiff ball of dough, about 2 minutes. Remove from heat.
4. Add 1 egg and beat strongly until dough is shiny and smooth. Add remaining egg and again beat strongly until dough is shiny and smooth.
5. Drop dough by tablespoonfuls onto a greased cookie sheet and shape into strips about 1 inch wide and 4 inches long. Space strips about 2 inches apart.
6. Bake on the middle shelf of oven at 425° F for 25 to 30 minutes, until puffed and golden brown. Remove pastry shells from oven, place on wire racks, and let cool.
7. Split shells lengthwise and, if necessary, remove some of the

inside pastry dough, and fill with Cream Filling. Top with a thick layer of Chocolate Frosting.

Yield: 6 to 8 éclairs

CREAM FILLING
⅔ cup sugar
5 tablespoons flour
Dash salt
2 cups milk
2 eggs, beaten
1 teaspoon vanilla extract

1. Combine sugar, flour, and salt in a heavy saucepan. Slowly mix in milk. Cook over low heat, stirring constantly, until mixture comes to a boil and then boil for 1 minute. Remove from heat.

2. Stir ¼ cup of the hot milk mixture into eggs, blending well, and then pour eggs into remaining milk mixture. Heat just to boiling, stirring constantly. Remove from heat.

3. Cover pan with towel and let cool. Blend in vanilla.

CHOCOLATE FROSTING
1 ounce unsweetened baking
   chocolate
1 tablespoon butter or margarine
¾ cup sifted confectioners' sugar
1 tablespoon boiling water

Melt chocolate and butter over hot water. Add sugar and water, stirring until mixture is smooth and well blended.

CHILE □ The Juan Fernandez Islands, located in the Pacific Ocean 400 miles west of the South American mainland, are part of Chile.

These islands are popularly known as the Robinson Crusoe Islands because a Scottish sailor named Alexander Selkirk lived there as a castaway between 1705 and 1709. Selkirk's adventure inspired Daniel Defoe to write his classic story about Robinson Crusoe's experiences on a deserted island.

Easter Island, another Pacific island of great interest, was annexed by Chile in 1888. Easter Island is about 2,200 miles west of Chile and

28

is well known for its massive carved stone head statues and unusual hieroglyphs.

COLOMBIA

2 cups hulled strawberries
2 cups sugar
1 egg white, stiffly beaten
2 cups heavy cream, stiffly whipped
1 cup confectioners' sugar

Strawberry Mousse

Here is a cool and refreshing dessert that is a nice change from ice cream or sherbet, and it can be enjoyed throughout the year.

1. Crush strawberries and combine with sugar in a heavy saucepan. Cook over low heat, stirring, until sugar dissolves. Do not boil.
2. Remove from heat and chill in refrigerator.
3. Fold egg white and whipped cream into strawberry mixture. Thoroughly fold in confectioners' sugar.
4. Spoon mousse into a 2-quart dish or an open container and freeze at least 24 hours before serving.

Yield: 8 to 10 servings

COLOMBIA □ The Gold Museum in Bogotá, Colombia, certainly lives up to its name. There are more than 35,000 gold artifacts on display dating from before the time of Christopher Columbus, including religious and ceremonial objects, royal crowns, rings, necklaces, and pendants.

In addition to this dazzling display of gold, the museum also has a very large collection of emeralds, including the largest unpolished gemstone in the world.

ECUADOR

3 egg yolks, beaten
2 cups flour
1 tablespoon butter or margarine,
   melted
Dash salt
1 cup milk
1 teaspoon baking powder
3 tablespoons brandy
½ teaspoon anise extract
Cooking oil
Brown Sugar Syrup (recipe follows)

Anise Brandy Crullers

These delicious crullers with a light crispy crust will show you that there is a lot more adventure in eating doughnuts than just having a hole in the center or a spoonful of jelly inside.

1. Mix together egg yolks, flour, butter, and salt. Gradually add milk, stirring well. Mix in baking powder, brandy, and anise extract until well blended.
2. Heat the oil to very hot and drop dough by tablespoonfuls into oil. Fry until crullers are a deep golden brown. Remove from oil and drain on paper towels.
3. Pour warm Brown Sugar Syrup over top.
Yield: approximately 30 crullers,

BROWN SUGAR SYRUP
1 cup packed brown sugar
¼ cup water
¼ teaspoon ground cinnamon
¼ teaspoon vanilla extract

Cook sugar and water over medium heat, stirring constantly, until sugar dissolves and mixture just comes to a boil. Remove from heat and stir in cinnamon and vanilla.

ECUADOR □ One of the most notable exports from Ecuador has brought little recognition to that country because of a misunderstanding that has persisted for over one hundred years.

For many years high-quality *toquilla* straw from Ecuador has been used to make straw hats that have been popular all over the world. When these hats were first made in the 1800s, however, most of them were shipped to Panama, both for customers there and for reshipment to other parts of the world. Because these fine Ecuadorian hats appeared to have originated in Panama, they became known as "Panama hats."

PARAGUAY

4 cups flour
1¼ cups sugar
½ tablespoon baking powder
Dash salt
1 teaspoon grated lemon peel
¼ cup butter or margarine, softened
1 egg, beaten
1 teaspoon lemon juice
½ cup milk
Chocolate Cream Filling
   (recipe follows)
Caramel Sauce (recipe follows)
Oatmeal Topping (recipe follows)

Cream-Filled Cookie Cake

When you cannot decide whether you want a cookie or a cake to finish your meal, this dessert offers the best combination of both. The cake layers are crunchy just like cookies and the cream filling and the two toppings make it a delicious cake.

1. Preheat oven to 400° F.
2. Sift together flour, sugar, baking powder, and salt. Mix in lemon peel. Add butter, mixing with fingers to a bread crumb consistency. Add egg, lemon juice, and milk, kneading well.
3. Divide dough into five equal parts. Roll out each part into a circle about 10 inches in diameter.
4. Place circles on greased cookie sheets and bake at 400° F for 6 to 8 minutes, until lightly browned. Let cool.
5. Stack cake layers, spreading each layer with warm Chocolate Cream Filling. Pour Caramel Sauce over top and then sprinkle with Oatmeal Topping.
6. Chill in refrigerator for at least 3 hours before serving. Store in refrigerator.

Yield: 8 to 10 servings

CHOCOLATE CREAM FILLING

3 tablespoons cornstarch
⅓ cup sugar
3 tablespoons cocoa powder
2 egg yolks, lightly beaten
2 cups milk
1 teaspoon vanilla extract

1. Combine cornstarch, sugar, cocoa powder, and egg yolks, mixing together well. Set aside.
2. Heat milk over hot water. Gradually add cocoa mixture and continue to cook, stirring constantly, until mixture thickens.
3. Remove from heat and stir in vanilla.

CARAMEL SAUCE

1 cup brown sugar
1 cup granulated sugar
⅔ cup water

Combine sugars and water in a heavy saucepan and cook over medium heat, stirring constantly, until sugar dissolves. Bring to a boil and let boil for 10 minutes without stirring. Let cool slightly.

OATMEAL TOPPING

2 tablespoons butter or margarine
⅓ cup sugar
⅓ cup oatmeal

Melt butter over medium heat. Add sugar and oatmeal and cook, stirring constantly, until mixture becomes lightly browned.

PARAGUAY □ In many countries the original native languages are abandoned in favor of the supposedly more sophisticated and socially acceptable languages introduced into the country by outsiders. But this is not the case in Paraguay.

Although Spanish is the official language of the country, brought there hundreds of years ago by explorers and colonizers, most people in Paraguay still speak the Guarani Indian language of their ancestors. In fact, it is considered a status symbol to speak the native language and any politician seeking a successful career must be able to speak Guarani fluently.

PERU

1 can (14 ounces) sweetened
  condensed milk
1 can (12 ounces) evaporated milk
1 cup sugar
1 teaspoon vanilla extract
8 egg yolks, beaten
Meringue Floats (recipe follows)
Ground cinnamon

Vanilla Pudding with Meringue Floats

This dessert is known in Peru as "Remembrances of Lima," and even if you never get to visit that South American country you will create your own memories with this delicate custard and unique wine-flavored meringue.

1. Mix together milks, sugar, and vanilla in a heavy pan and cook over medium heat, stirring constantly with a wooden spoon, until mixture begins to thicken. Remove from heat.

2. Add egg yolks to milk mixture and cook again over medium heat for 2 to 3 minutes, stirring constantly. Pour custard into a serving bowl and let cool.

3. Drop Meringue Floats by tablespoonfuls onto the custard. Sprinkle cinnamon over top.

Yield: 8 to 10 servings

MERINGUE FLOATS

1½ cups sugar
1 cup port wine
4 egg whites, stiffly beaten

1. Mix together sugar and wine in a saucepan and heat to boiling. Let boil for 3 minutes without stirring.

2. Slowly beat the sugar and wine syrup into the beaten egg whites until thoroughly mixed.

PERU □ Archaeologists are beginning to make detailed studies of Gran Pajaten, a "lost city" recently discovered in the jungle on the eastern slopes of the Andes Mountains in Peru.

There are stone buildings, statues, walls, and burial towers that could date as far back as A.D. 500. One of the most interesting things about Gran Pajaten is that the inhabitants had an established agriculture as indicated by the terraced fields cut into the surrounding hillsides. Since the area has too much rain for any crop today, a study of the fields might reveal what types of foods were grown by these people so long ago, their cultural and economic activities, and their ties to other ancient peoples of the Andes.

SURINAME

4 bananas
1 cup flour
½ teaspoon baking soda
Dash salt
¾ cup water
Cooking oil

Fried Bananas

Here is a new banana taste treat for people who enjoy this popular fruit from South America.

1. Peel and slice bananas lengthwise. Set aside.
2. Combine flour, baking soda, salt, and water, mixing together well. Dip banana slices into batter and let excess drip off.
3. Heat oil and fry bananas until golden brown. Drain on paper towels.

Yield: 4 servings

SURINAME □ Suriname, known as Dutch Guiana before gaining independence in November 1975, is a small country in northeastern South America with a very diversified and cosmopolitan population.

The people of Suriname include Blacks, Creoles, Asian Indians, East Indians, American Indians, Chinese, Javanese, and Europeans, with each group preserving its own culture, religion, and language.

URUGUAY

3 cups flour
5 teaspoons baking powder
¾ cup sugar
¾ cup butter or margarine, softened
2 eggs, beaten
¼ cup milk
2 cups quince jelly
1 egg yolk

Quince Torte

This torte is a traditional favorite in Uruguay and offers a new taste with a jelly that is not commonly used.

1. Preheat oven to 350° F.
2. Sift together flour, baking powder, and sugar. Add butter, eggs, and milk, kneading well. Add additional milk if necessary, a tablespoon at a time, to make a workable dough. Set aside one quarter of the dough.
3. Roll out remaining dough into a circle 10 inches in diameter. Place into a greased, deep 9-inch pan, with the dough overlapping the sides. Spoon quince jelly into pie pan.
4. Roll out remaining quarter of the dough, cut into strips, and place over jelly in a crisscross pattern. Crimp ends of the strips to the pie crust. Brush strips with egg yolk.
5. Bake at 350° F for 25 to 30 minutes, until crust is lightly browned.
Yield: 8 to 10 servings.

URUGUAY ☐ The people of Uruguay eat a great deal of meat, especially beef cooked over open fires. There are restaurants, called *parrilladas*, throughout the country that serve almost nothing but meat prepared on charcoal grills.

Many of the men who work outdoors in construction and along the highways, rather than bringing sandwiches with them in lunch boxes, will make a fire and grill steaks for their midday meal.

VENEZUELA

1½ cups coconut milk
9 egg yolks
Dash salt
½ cup water
1¾ cups sugar
8 slices poundcake
2 tablespoons cognac mixed with
   2 tablespoons water
Ground cinnamon

Coconut Milk Cognac Cake

This easy no-bake cake, with a strong cognac flavor and a creamy coconut milk custard filling, turns plain poundcake into a dessert for special occasions.

1. Mix together coconut milk, egg yolks, and salt. Set aside.
2. Combine water and sugar in a heavy saucepan and cook over medium-high heat, stirring until sugar dissolves. Let boil, without stirring, for 5 to 6 minutes.
3. Remove from heat and add coconut milk mixture, stirring until mixture becomes creamy. Cook over low heat, stirring constantly, until mixture just begins to boil. Remove from heat, let cool slightly, and divide into three equal portions.
4. Spoon one third of the coconut milk custard evenly into the bottom of a 9x13-inch baking dish. Place 4 slices of poundcake over the custard, forming a cake layer. Mix the cognac with the water and sprinkle half of the cognac and water mixture evenly over poundcake

slices. Spoon another third of the coconut milk custard over the pound-cake layer and place the other 4 slices of poundcake on top. Sprinkle remaining cognac and water mixture over top and then cover with remaining coconut milk custard. Sprinkle with cinnamon.

5. Chill in refrigerator and serve cold.

Yield: 8 servings.

VENEZUELA □ Ardent skiers will find exceptional opportunities to enjoy their sport in the Sierra Nevada National Park in northwestern Venezuela.

There are ski slopes in the park at an altitude of fourteen thousand feet, and they can be used for six months of the year, from June through November.

WESTERN EUROPE

AUSTRIA

5 ounces sweet chocolate
1 tablespoon water
¾ cup butter or margarine
6 egg yolks, beaten
1 cup confectioners' sugar
1¼ cups flour
6 egg whites, stiffly beaten
⅓ cup apricot jam
Chocolate Icing (recipe follows)

Sacher Torte

If countries had an official national cake, this chocolate and jam cake would certainly be Austria's.

1. Preheat oven to 325° F.
2. Break chocolate into small pieces and heat over hot water until melted. Add water and butter and stir until butter melts and mixture is smooth and well blended. Add egg yolks, beating constantly. Mix in sugar. Remove from heat and let cool for 10 minutes.
3. Thoroughly but gently fold chocolate mixture alternately with flour into beaten egg whites.
4. Spoon batter into a greased 8-inch square pan that has been dusted with flour. Bake at 325° F for 30 minutes, until cake tests clean. Remove from pan and set aside to cool.
5. Heat jam over hot water, stirring until jam has melted. Spread over top of cake and let set for about 20 minutes. Spread Chocolate Icing over cake.

Yield: 6 to 8 servings

CHOCOLATE ICING

3 ounces unsweetened chocolate
¾ cup confectioners' sugar
2 tablespoons hot water
1 egg, beaten
1 egg yolk, beaten
5 tablespoons butter or margarine,
softened

Melt chocolate over hot water. Remove from heat and add sugar and water, mixing together well. Add egg and beat briskly. Add egg yolk, beating well. Add butter, one tablespoon at a time, beating steadily until mixture is smooth.

AUSTRIA □ Although Austria and its capital city of Vienna are most often associated with Johann Strauss and his waltzes, the country has been home to the greatest composers of Europe. Some of them were born and worked in Austria, while others were born elsewhere and came there to create their music.

The list of these giants of music who made Austria their home includes Wolfgang Amadeus Mozart, Ludwig van Beethoven, Gustav Mahler, Josef Haydn, Franz Schubert, Johannes Brahms, and Anton Bruckner.

BELGIUM

2 cups water
1½ tablespoons dry yeast
4 cups flour
4 egg yolks
½ cup sugar
2 cups milk
½ cup plus 2 tablespoons butter or
  margarine, melted
½ teaspoon salt
1 tablespoon oil
1 teaspoon vanilla extract
4 egg whites, stiffly beaten
Whipped cream
Sliced fruit
Confectioners' sugar

Belgian Waffles

Belgian waffles are a special treat known all over the world but usually available only at a World's Fair or at a seaside resort. Now you can make these waffles at home and enjoy them whenever you want, which will be often.

1. Warm ½ cup of the water and stir in yeast. Set aside to let yeast dissolve.
2. Place flour in a large bowl and mix in egg yolks, sugar, and softened yeast. Add remaining 1½ cups water, milk, butter, salt, oil, and vanilla, mixing until smooth. Fold in egg whites.
3. Let stand for about 1 hour, stirring every 15 minutes.
4. Pour batter into a waffle iron and cook as for regular waffles.
5. Top with whipped cream and fruit slices and sprinkle with confectioners' sugar.
Yield: approximately 16 waffles

BELGIUM □ Pigeon racing is a very popular sport in Belgium, with some races crossing international borders and starting as far away as Spain and southern France. It is quite common to hear on the radio in Belgium reports of weather conditions along the routes of major races.

The Grand'Place (the central place) in Brussels is the site of a weekly pigeon market where birds are bought and sold, and it takes a large amount of money to become the owner of a good racer.

ENGLAND

1 poundcake (about 12 ounces)
¼ cup raspberry preserve
1 cup blanched almonds, split in
   halves
½ cup sherry
½ cup raspberry brandy
2 cups heavy cream
2 tablespoons superfine sugar
2 cups fresh raspberries, or 2 10-
   ounce packages frozen raspberries,
   defrosted and completely drained
Custard Sauce (recipe follows)

Trifle

Although the dictionary will say that a "trifle" is something of little worth, the English place a great deal of value on this delicious cake and fruit dessert.

1. Cut poundcake into 1-inch slices and spread with raspberry preserve. Place two or three slices of cake, preserve side up, in the bottom of a glass serving bowl 9 inches across and at least 3 inches high.

2. Cut remaining slices of cake into 1-inch cubes and scatter them over the cake slices already in bowl. Sprinkle ½ cup of the almonds over top. Pour in sherry and brandy and set aside to soak for at least 30 minutes.

3. Whip cream until it thickens slightly. Add sugar and continue to beat until mixture becomes very stiff. Set aside.

4. Spread 1¾ cups of raspberries over cake in bowl. Spread Custard Sauce over top. Gently spoon whipped cream over Custard Sauce.

5. Pile remaining ¼ cup of raspberries in center and sprinkle remaining ½ cup of almonds around raspberries.

6. It is best to serve this dessert immediately, but it can be kept in the refrigerator an hour or two before serving.

Yield: 6 to 8 servings

CUSTARD SAUCE

2 tablespoons cornstarch
1 cup sugar
2 cups milk, scalded
4 egg yolks, slightly beaten
1 teaspoon vanilla extract

1. Mix cornstarch and sugar. Stir in milk. Pour mixture over egg yolks.

2. Cook over hot water, stirring constantly, until mixture thickens. Remove from heat and let cool. Stir in vanilla.

ENGLAND □ At an international conference of astronomers held in Washington, D.C., in 1884, it was decided that a north-south line passing through the Royal Observatory in Greenwich, a borough of London, would be the Prime Meridian—the meridian of zero longitude. The Greenwich Meridian also designates Greenwich Mean Time —the base line that is used to establish time zones around the world.

The Royal Observatory was moved out of Greenwich about thirty years ago because of interference from the lights of London, but there is still much to see in the borough. Among the many historic buildings are the National Maritime Museum, the Royal Naval College with buildings designed by Christopher Wren, and the Queen's House designed by Inigo Jones, one of England's first great architects.

Along the Thames River waterfront there are two ships of particular historic interest: the *Cutty Sark*, the last of the great clipper ships that sailed between England and the Orient, and the *Gipsy Moth IV*, the

small sailboat in which Sir Francis Chichester sailed around the world
alone in 1966–1967 at the age of sixty-six.

FRANCE

1½ cups sugar
6 egg yolks
½ cup flour
2 cups hot milk
1 teaspoon vanilla extract
2 tablespoons butter or margarine,
 softened
3 tablespoons rum
1 cup apricot jam
Crust (recipe follows)
Sliced fresh fruit (bananas, apricots,
 strawberries, peaches, plums, etc.)

French Tart

*Even if this tart were the only food to come from France, French cooking
would still have a fabulous reputation. This dessert is a delight to look
at as well as to eat.*

   1. Gradually add 1 cup of the sugar to egg yolks, mixing well. Add
flour and beat until mixture becomes thick, smooth, and pale yellow.
Very gradually add hot milk, stirring well.
   2. Pour mixture into a heavy saucepan and cook over medium heat,
stirring constantly with a whisk, until it just begins to boil. Reduce
heat and simmer for 3 to 4 minutes more, stirring constantly. Mixture
will be very thick.
   3. Remove from heat and add vanilla and butter, mixing well. Pour
rum over top and chill in refrigerator.
   4. Combine apricot jam and remaining ½ cup of sugar in a heavy
saucepan and cook over medium heat, stirring constantly, until mixture becomes syrupy and begins to boil.

5. Brush half of apricot jam syrup over entire Crust. Evenly spoon chilled custard filling into Crust. Top with slices of fresh fruit. Brush tart with remaining apricot jam syrup.

6. Chill in refrigerator and serve tart the same day it is made.

Yield: 6 servings

CRUST

1½ cups flour
½ teaspoon baking powder
½ teaspoon salt
½ cup shortening, melted
¼ cup cold water
1 teaspoon vanilla extract

1. Preheat oven to 450° F.

2. Combine flour, baking powder, salt, shortening, water, and vanilla, mixing together well.

3. Roll out dough on a floured surface into an approximately 8x12-inch rectangle. Fold up edges of dough to make a 1-inch side all around. Prick bottom of dough several times with a fork.

4. Carefully place crust on a greased cookie sheet and bake at 450° F for 10 to 12 minutes, until golden brown.

FRANCE □ For eleven years, from 1925 to 1936, the Eiffel Tower in Paris carried the largest advertising sign ever made.

A quarter of a million electric bulbs in six colors spelled out in vertical lettering the name *Citroën*, advertising the French automobile manufacturer with lights that could be seen twenty-five miles away.

GERMANY

Juice of 1 lemon
3 tablespoons brandy
½ cup plus 3 tablespoons sugar
6 apples
3 egg whites
3 egg yolks
3 tablespoons flour
⅛ teaspoon baking powder
1 teaspoon vanilla extract
1 tablespoon confectioners' sugar
¼ cup milk
½ cup unsalted butter or margarine
1 tablespoon ground cinnamon
Vanilla Sauce (recipe follows)

Fried Apple Slices in Vanilla Sauce

Eating an apple a day is easy when the apple is made into this buttery treat with brandy, lemon, and cinnamon sugar.

1. Combine lemon juice, brandy, and 1 tablespoon of the sugar, mixing together well. Set aside.
2. Peel and core apples and slice into ½-inch thick rings. Soak apple rings in brandy mixture. Set aside.
3. Beat together egg whites and 2 tablespoons of the sugar until stiff. Gently mix in egg yolks, flour, baking powder, vanilla, and confectioners' sugar. Stir in milk.
4. Melt butter in a heavy pan, dip apple rings into batter, and fry apple rings in butter until golden brown.
5. Remove apple rings from pan, drain, and place on serving plate. Combine remaining ½ cup sugar and cinnamon and sprinkle over fried apple rings. Serve with warm Vanilla Sauce.

Yield: 4 to 6 servings

(continued)

VANILLA SAUCE
2 *tablespoons butter or margarine*
2 *tablespoons flour*
1 *cup boiling water*
2 *tablespoons sugar*
1 *tablespoon vanilla extract*

1. Melt butter in heavy pan, add flour, and continue heating, while stirring, until mixture bubbles. Add water and sugar, stirring constantly, and cook until smooth.

2. Remove from heat and add vanilla, mixing together well.

GERMANY □ Frankfurt, West Germany, is a major industrial, transportation, financial, commercial, and educational center not only for Germany, but for all of Europe.

The city is also very important in the publishing industry with roots that go back hundreds of years. Johann Gutenberg, the inventor of movable type, opened a shop in Frankfurt in 1454; the *Frankfurter Allgemeine Zeitung* is one of the great newspapers of the world; and the annual Frankfurt Book Fair is the largest of its kind.

Pink Elephant under Pear Tree, Anonymous, Poland. UNICEF card issued in 1984.

The Little Island, by Fernando Fantini, Italy. UNICEF card issued in 1977.

Festival in Orange, by
Grand'Mère Paris, France.
UNICEF card issued in 1982.

Children Playing, by Samantha Elias, Brazil. UNICEF
card issued in 1980.

IRELAND

½ cup butter or margarine, softened
2 cups ground almonds
¼ cup sugar
1 tablespoon brandy
¼ teaspoon orange flower water
2 egg whites, stiffly beaten
Blanched almonds
Carrot or celery leaves

Almond Meringue Rocks

The green decorations around the base of this meringue dessert are there to resemble plants, such as shamrocks, growing among the rocks in Ireland.

1. Heat a mixing bowl by pouring boiling water in it and then emptying all the water out. Combine butter, ground almonds, and sugar in the mixing bowl and mix together well. Add brandy and orange flower water, beating continuously, until bowl cools off completely. Fold in egg whites.
2. Chill in refrigerator overnight. Mixture will be soft but firm. Break into rough pieces and pile into a pyramid on a serving dish.
3. Sprinkle blanched almonds over pyramid and garnish base with carrot or celery leaves.

Yield: 4 servings

IRELAND □ Donegal in northwestern Ireland was an early Viking settlement and gets its name from the Irish words *Dun Nan Gall*, meaning "Fort of the Foreigners."

Today the name Donegal means some of the finest tweed clothing anywhere in the world. Donegal tweed is handmade by residents of the area who weave the cloth at home, continuing a craft that is hundreds of years old in that part of Ireland. Although the weaving work itself goes back many years, a great revival in the craft around 1900 brought new prosperity to the Donegal area, which had been suffering severe economic hardship.

ITALY

2 cups flour
1 tablespoon dry yeast
⅔ cup warm water
3 eggs
¾ cup butter or margarine, softened
Dash salt
1 tablespoon sugar
⅓ cup seedless raisins
Rum Syrup (recipe follows)

Rum Baba

This light cake is not too sweet so that you can also serve it as a bread with meals.

1. Mix together 1¼ cups of the flour, yeast, and warm water. Cover and let sit in a warm place for about 15 minutes, until dough doubles in size.
2. Put raised dough in a large bowl and add remaining ¾ cup flour, eggs, butter, and salt. Knead until dough becomes smooth, velvety, and elastic. Additional flour can be added, if necessary. Knead in sugar and raisins.
3. Place dough in a 1½ quart greased tubular cake pan. The dough will fill about one third of the pan. Let sit in a warm place for about 1½ hours, until dough rises to top of pan.
4. Preheat oven to 425° F.
5. Bake at 425° F for about 25 minutes, until toothpick tests clean.

6. Remove from cake pan, turn over into a deep dish, and pour Rum Syrup over cake. Baste with Rum Syrup as cake cools.

Yield: 8 to 10 servings.

RUM SYRUP
½ *cup water*
3 *tablespoons sugar*
½ *cup rum*

Combine water and sugar in a small saucepan and heat to boiling. Let boil for 3 minutes. Remove from heat and stir in rum.

ITALY □ Twice in the last seven hundred years notable historic events have taken place in the small Italian village of Larderello, which sits in the Tuscany hills about forty miles southwest of Florence.

There are a number of hot springs clustered around Larderello, and in the early fourteenth century the sight of the escaping jets of super-heated steam—at temperatures as high as 375° F shooting two hundred feet up into the air—inspired Dante's vision of Inferno.

The second historic event occurred around 1910 when wells were drilled into the underground pockets of hot steam and the steam was piped up and passed through turbine generators. This was the first time that geothermal energy had ever been used to produce electricity.

LUXEMBOURG

1 cup butter or margarine, softened
1⅔ cups confectioners' sugar
6 eggs
6½ cups flour
Dash salt
¼ cup rum
Grated peel of 1 lemon
½ teaspoon baking powder
Cooking oil
Confectioners' sugar

Bowtie Cookies

Luxembourg is one of the smallest countries in Europe, but these attractive and lightly fried crispy cookies will become one of your biggest favorites.

1. Cream butter. Gradually add 1⅔ cups confectioners' sugar, eggs, flour, salt, rum, grated lemon peel, and baking powder, mixing together well. Batter will be stiff.
2. Chill in refrigerator for 1 hour.
3. Roll out dough to ⅛-inch thickness on a lightly floured surface. Cut into strips about 5 inches long and ½ inch wide.
4. Heat oil to very hot. Tie strips into loose knots and deep fry, a few at a time, for 1 to 2 minutes, until golden brown. Remove with a slotted spoon and drain on paper towels.
5. Sprinkle with confectioners' sugar.
Yield: approximately 3½ dozen cookies

LUXEMBOURG □ The people of the Grand Duchy of Luxembourg have a motto—"We wish to remain what we are"—that clearly shows their desire for independence and confidence in their way of life. This motto is very much reflected in the use of the native language, Letzeburgisch.

Although German and French were designated the national languages of the country in 1830, the people of Luxembourg continued to speak Letzeburgisch so that it, too, was added as an official language in 1939.

Even in such a small country—Luxembourg is only 51 miles from north to south and thirty-five miles wide at its greatest width—there are variations in the way Letzeburgisch is spoken. And its grammar is so vague that little effort has been made to put the language into print.

NETHERLANDS

4 cups milk
½ cup rice
Dash salt
2 teaspoons vanilla extract
⅔ cup sugar
2 tablespoons (two ¼-ounce envelopes) unflavored gelatin softened in ½ cup water
2 cups dried apricots
3 tablespoons sugar
4 large egg whites, stiffly beaten
1 cup heavy cream, whipped

Apricot Rice Pudding

Only a small amount of rice is used in this pudding, more for texture than for taste, allowing the apricot flavor to reach its peak.

1. Combine milk, rice, salt, and vanilla in a saucepan and cook over low heat, stirring often, for about 20 minutes, until rice is done. Add sugar and stir until dissolved. Remove from heat. Stir softened gelatin into rice. Set aside to cool and let stand until slightly firm.

2. Place apricots in a saucepan, cover with water, add sugar, and simmer until apricots become soft.

3. Remove from heat, drain apricots, and save liquid. Divide apricots into 3 equal parts. Set aside.

4. Fold egg whites into rice mixture. Fold in whipped cream.

5. Rinse a 2-quart mold with cold water. Spread a layer of rice pudding in the bottom. Spread one third of the apricots on top, leaving a ½-inch ring around the edge. Spread a second layer of rice pudding over the apricots and then another third of the apricots, again leaving a ½-inch ring around the edge. Cover with remaining rice pudding.

6. Chill in refrigerator until completely set.

7. Force remaining apricots through a strainer and mix pulp with the juice set aside from cooking the apricots.

8. Remove rice pudding from mold and pour apricot sauce around base.

Yield: 6 to 8 servings

NETHERLANDS □ Amsterdam is an especially delightful city for visitors. There are more than fifty canals and five hundred bridges; picturesque gabled brick houses dating from the 1600s and the 1700s stand along the canals; interesting shops line Kalverstraat, the main shopping street; paintings by Rembrandt, including his *Night Watch*, are in the Rijksmuseum; the works of Van Gogh are in the Stedelijk Museum; and performances can be heard by the world-renowned Concert-gebouw Orchestra.

But for many people the highlight of the city will be a look at one of Amsterdam's oldest industries: the cutting and polishing of diamonds. Amsterdam is the leading diamond market in the world and some of the diamond companies offer tours for visitors to see the craftsmen working on the sparkling stones.

SCOTLAND

1 cup finely crushed bread crumbs
⅔ cup plus 1 tablespoon sugar
3 egg yolks, beaten
2 cups milk
1 teaspoon grated lemon peel
2 tablespoons butter or margarine,
    melted
3 tablespoons warm apricot or
    raspberry jam
3 egg whites, stiffly beaten

Bread and Jam Pudding

The mystical village of Brigadoon in Scotland appears only once every hundred years, but, fortunately, you can enjoy whenever you want this Scottish treat that combines a meringue topping with a sweet fruit-flavored bread filling.

1. Preheat oven to 350° F.
2. Combine bread crumbs, ⅓ cup of the sugar, egg yolks, milk, and lemon peel, mixing well. Blend in butter.
3. Spoon mixture into a greased 1½-quart ovenware dish. Bake at 350° F for about 50 minutes, until set.
4. Remove from oven and immediately spread jam over top. Set aside.
5. Fold ⅓ cup of the remaining sugar into egg whites. Pile mixture over jam. Sprinkle lightly with remaining tablespoon of sugar.
6. Bake at 350° F for about 10 minutes, or until meringue is golden brown.

Yield: 6 to 8 servings

SCOTLAND □ Golf probably developed in Scotland around 1100 from a Roman game called *paganica*, which used a bent stick to hit a leather ball stuffed with feathers across the open countryside. The word *golf* comes from the Germanic word for "club."

Whatever the early origins of the game, there is general agreement that the true home of present-day golf is St. Andrews in Scotland. It was at the Royal and Ancient Golf Club of St. Andrews, founded in 1754 and the oldest golf club in continuous existence, that the specific rules of the game were drawn up, including the regulation eighteen-hole course.

SWITZERLAND

1 cup finely chopped almonds
1 cup confectioners' sugar
2 egg whites
2 egg yolks, lightly beaten
Juice of half a lemon
Confectioners' sugar
Icing (recipe follows)

Crisp Almond Squares

The Swiss have worked hard over the years to preserve their neutrality in the world, but you will be on their side in a minute after trying these dainty almond cookies. They are especially good with a small dish of ice cream or served with a late night cup of coffee or tea.

1. Combine almonds, sugar, and egg whites and heat over hot water until mixture becomes very thick and leaves side of pan. Remove from heat and mix in egg yolks and lemon juice.

2. Roll out dough to ¼-inch thickness on a surface covered with confectioners' sugar. Cut into 1-inch squares, place on a cookie sheet,

and sprinkle with confectioners' sugar. Let stand uncovered in a warm place for 24 hours.

3. Bake for about 15 minutes in a preheated 350° F oven and immediately brush with Icing.

Yield: approximately 6 dozen cookies

ICING
¾ cup confectioners' sugar
1 egg white
Juice of 1 lemon

Beat together well sugar, egg white, and lemon juice.

SWITZERLAND □ Switzerland used the 1939–1940 World's Fair in New York City to introduce one of its great national treasures to the people of America.

Steaming crocks of cheese fondue heated over small flames were served in the Swiss Pavilion to eager visitors who first hesitantly, and then enthusiastically, dipped long-handled forks stuck with small squares of bread into the gently bubbling mixture of Emmentaler and Gruyère cheeses, garlic, flour, white wine, and kirsch.

IBERIA

PORTUGAL

6 ounces semisweet chocolate
1 teaspoon instant coffee powder
1 teaspoon butter or margarine
2 tablespoons port wine
6 egg yolks, beaten
2 tablespoons sugar
6 egg whites, stiffly beaten
Whipped cream

Chocolate Mousse

Even though there are many different recipes for making chocolate mousse, the Portuguese have the right idea when they make their special version with port wine.

1. Combine chocolate, coffee powder, and butter and melt over hot water, stirring until mixture is smooth and well blended. Add wine. Add egg yolks and sugar, stirring until mixture thickens. Turn off heat but leave mixture over hot water.
2. Fold in egg whites and stir until mixture becomes soft and creamy.
3. Spoon mousse into individual serving dishes, let cool slightly, and then chill in the refrigerator.
4. Top with whipped cream just before serving.
Yield: 4 to 6 servings

PORTUGAL □ Ten percent of all the farmland in Portugal is used for vineyards.

Port wine is made from grapes grown in the Douro Valley near the coastal city of Porto in northern Portugal. The grapes from the Madeiras, the Portuguese islands in the Atlantic Ocean about five hundred miles southwest of Portugal, are used to make Madeira wine.

The vineyards in the southern part of the country grow grapes for eating.

SPAIN

½ cup sliced almonds
½ cup Madeira wine
1 sponge cake layer, 8 inches in
   diameter
6 eggs, beaten
2 cups milk
1 cup sugar
¼ teaspoon ground cinnamon
½ cup shaved chocolate

Madeira Custard Cake

For those of you who prefer to eat your wine rather than drink it, this Madeira-soaked cake is just the thing.

1. Preheat oven to 325° F.

2. To toast almonds, spread on an ungreased cookie sheet and bake at 325° F for 12 minutes. Set aside.

3. Drizzle wine over cake. Spread toasted almonds over top. Set aside.

4. Combine eggs, milk, sugar, and cinnamon in a heavy pan. Slowly heat over hot, not boiling, water, stirring gently, until custard becomes very thick and just begins to bubble. Remove from heat and let cool.

5. Spoon custard over cake and sprinkle with chocolate.

Yield: 8 to 10 servings.

SPAIN □ Historic Toledo is located in central Spain about forty miles south of the capital of Madrid. The city sits on a hill surrounded by a deep ravine through which the Tagus River flows.

Toledo has so many art treasures and buildings of architectural and historic interest that the entire city has been declared a Spanish national monument. Toledo's heritage includes the magnificent Gothic cathedral dating from the mid-1200s; El Greco's home and many of his paintings; the El Tránsito Synagogue from 1366; and the Church of San Juan de los Reyes, built by King Ferdinand and Queen Isabella in 1477.

In addition to all these points of interest, there are spectacular panoramic views of Toledo from the opposite bank of the Tagus River.

SCANDINAVIA

DENMARK

¾ cup butter or margarine, softened
2 cups flour
3 tablespoons sugar
1 egg yolk
Vanilla Cream (recipe follows)
Icing (recipe follows)
Jelly

VANILLA CREAM
2 eggs
2 tablespoons sugar
2 tablespoons wheat flour
1 teaspoon vanilla extract
1¼ cups cream

Iced Sandwich Cookies

It is a good idea to make a double or triple batch of these neat looking cookies because they will disappear like magic when you put them out.

1. Preheat oven to 400° F.
2. Mix together butter and flour. Add sugar and egg yolk and knead until dough becomes smooth. Let sit in a cool place for about 2 hours.
3. Roll out dough to ⅛-inch thickness. Cut into circles with round cookie cutter or a drinking glass.
4. Place on a greased cookie sheet 2 inches apart and bake at 400° F for about 10 minutes. Let cool on racks.
5. Sandwich cookies with Vanilla Cream and cover top with Icing. Place about ½ teaspoon jelly on top of each cookie.
   Yield: approximately 15 cookies

1. Beat together eggs, sugar, flour, and vanilla. Set aside.
2. Heat cream in a heavy pan to boiling and pour into egg mixture. Stirring constantly, return egg and cream mixture to pan, bring to a boil, and continue to cook until mixture thickens. Remove from heat and let cool.

ICING

1 cup confectioners' sugar
1 to 2 tablespoons boiling water

Combine sugar and water and stir until icing is of spreading consistency.

DENMARK ☐ When Danish architect George Carstensen went to King Christian VIII in 1843 for support to build Tivoli Gardens on the old fortifications of the city of Copenhagen, he successfully persuaded the King by pointing out, "If people are allowed to amuse themselves, they will forget to talk politics."

The King agreed and Carstensen built the park a short time later, patterning it after Vauxhall Gardens in London. Over one hundred years later, in 1951, with Vauxhall Gardens long gone, the organizers of the Festival of Britain used Tivoli Gardens as the model for the Festival Gardens that were built in London.

FINLAND

2 eggs
¼ cup sugar
¾ cup heavy cream, whipped
½ cup flour
Dash salt
Jam

Cream Pancakes

The people of Finland get a double treat out of these rich pancakes. Besides enjoying them as a dessert with the jam topping, the Finns also sprinkle orange or lemon juice on top to make a special breakfast dish.

1. Preheat oven to 350° F.
2. Grease a 9-inch glass pie plate.
3. Beat eggs and sugar together until thick and foamy. Fold in whipped cream. Sift in flour and salt, stirring quickly. Pour immediately into the prepared pie plate.
4. Bake at 350° F for 30 to 40 minutes, until golden brown.
5. Let cool in a place free of drafts. Top with jam.
Yield: 4 to 6 servings

FINLAND □ It takes a special type of person to live and prosper in the harsh Arctic environment of Finland, and the people there have something special that they call *sisu*.

There is no exact translation for the word *sisu*, but it can best be described as a combination of the courage to endure and overcome unfavorable natural conditions, the determination to win mental and physical tests against a variety of hardships, and an outlook dominated by youthful vigor and optimism.

68

NORWAY

1¼ cups flour
1 teaspoon baking powder
1 cup butter or margarine, softened
1 cup sugar
4 large eggs
1 cup candied cherry halves
1 cup seedless grapes
½ cup slivered almonds
¼ teaspoon almond extract
Candied cherry halves
Slivered almonds

Cherry Almond Cake

Christmastime in Scandinavia sounds like a childhood fantasy and you can create a small part of that fantasy with the colorful fruit and rich flavor of this exceptional cake.

1. Preheat oven to 300° F.
2. Sift together flour and baking powder. Add butter, sugar, eggs, candied cherries, grapes, almonds, and almond extract, mixing together well.
3. Pour batter into a greased 8½-inch springform pan that has been lined with wax paper. Smooth out top of batter. Decorate top with candied cherries and almonds.
4. Bake at 300° F for 2¼ to 2½ hours.
5. Let cool for 15 minutes, remove from pan, and let cool completely.
Yield: 10 to 12 servings.

NORWAY □ The city of Oslo, the capital of Norway, is one of the largest cities in the world in land area, but unlike most metropolitan centers it is a city of great natural beauty with extensive areas of undeveloped land. In fact, more than two thirds of the city remains in its natural state of forests, meadows, and lakes.

69

Oslo did not experience the slow growth of many other large cities. In just one day, January 1, 1948, Oslo became twenty-seven times larger than it had been the day before. On that New Year's Day the city government, by decree, annexed enough surrounding land to make Oslo a major metropolis. Over the years, however, the unspoiled nature of the annexed lands has remained almost unchanged.

SWEDEN

¾ cup sugar
1⅓ cups ground hazelnuts
5 egg whites, stiffly beaten
3 rounded tablespoons cocoa powder
Butter Cream Frosting (recipe follows)
Toasted Almond Flakes (recipe
   follows)

Hazelnut Torte

Volvo cars, like this cake, are made in Sweden and they have a reputation for quality and longevity. This cake certainly has a reputation for quality but it will never have longevity. It is so good that every time you make it, this cake will be completely eaten within minutes.

1. Preheat oven to 300° F.
2. Fold sugar and hazelnuts into egg whites. Sift in cocoa powder.
3. Spread batter into two greased and floured 8-inch cake pans with removable bottoms. Bake at 300° F for about 35 minutes, until toothpick tests clean.
4. Remove from oven, remove sides of cake pans, and loosen cakes from bottom of pans while still warm. Let cool.
5. Stack cake layers, spreading Butter Cream Frosting between the

layers, over the top, and on the sides. Sprinkle with Toasted Almond Flakes.

Yield: 8 to 10 servings

BUTTER CREAM FROSTING
5 egg yolks, beaten
⅔ cup sugar
½ cup light cream
½ cup plus 3 tablespoons butter or margarine, softened

1. Combine egg yolks, sugar, and cream in a heavy saucepan and cook over low heat, stirring constantly and without boiling, until mixture thickens.
2. Remove from heat and stir until mixture cools slightly. Add butter, mixing until frosting is smooth. Chill in refrigerator until frosting has become thick enough to spread.

TOASTED ALMOND FLAKES
½ cup flaked almonds

1. Preheat oven to 350° F.
2. Spread almond flakes on an ungreased cookie sheet and bake at 350° F for 10 to 12 minutes.

SWEDEN □ The smorgasbord, a Swedish invention, is greatly enjoyed but very often improperly eaten. Despite the apparent freedom just to serve yourself in a random fashion from the abundant offerings, there is a definite order for partaking of the many different types of food on the *smorgasbordet*, the large serving table in the middle of the dining room.

According to tradition, the proper order for eating at a smorgasbord is as follows: begin with pickled herring and a boiled potato; then take some other fishes like Baltic Sea herring, sardines in oil, and smoked salmon; move on to the meat courses, including sliced beef, liver paste, and boiled ham; then a salad, fruit, and vegetable; and, in conclusion, some cheeses.

Sometimes a main dish is served after the smorgasbord but that may be passed up, going straight from the cheeses to dessert.

EASTERN EUROPE

CZECHOSLOVAKIA

Apple Strudel

3¼ cups flour
1 cup warm water
½ cup butter or margarine, melted
¼ cup sugar
Dash salt
1 egg
8 apples
Lemon juice
1½ tablespoons cinnamon mixed
    with ½ cup sugar
¾ cup raisins
1 cup chopped pecans
½ cup flaked coconut

This apple strudel is the kind of traditional family recipe that is handed down from generation to generation and will fill your house with the aroma of old-fashioned home baking.

1. Place flour in a large bowl and make a well in the middle. Add water, 2 tablespoons of the butter, ¼ cup of the sugar, salt, and egg. Mix together well.
2. Place dough on a floured surface and knead until it becomes easy to work. Divide into three parts and place each part in a small greased bowl. Cover with wax paper and a damp cloth. Set aside in a warm place.
3. Peel and core apples and cut into small pieces about ½ inch thick. Sprinkle with lemon juice to prevent their turning brown. Set aside.
4. Preheat oven to 375° F.
5. Roll out each portion of dough on a floured surface as thin as possible. Carefully lift dough, re-flour surface, and replace dough. Pushing with hands, stretch dough out as much as possible working from center to outside edges. Seal any holes.
6. Spread 4 tablespoons of the butter evenly on the three sheets of dough. Place apple pieces on dough sheets. Sprinkle 5 tablespoons

cinnamon sugar over apples. Sprinkle raisins, pecans, and coconut over top.

7. Roll up dough sheets and filling like a jelly roll. Brush top with remaining 2 tablespoons melted butter, sprinkle with remaining 3 tablespoons cinnamon sugar, and place all three rolls on a greased cookie sheet.

8. Bake at 375° F for about 45 minutes. Cut into thick slices and serve warm.

Yield: 6 to 8 servings

CZECHOSLOVAKIA □ Bohemianism was the name popularly given to the life style followed by artists, writers, and musicians. The Bohemian way of life was seen as being free, unconcerned about the future, and having little thought of material gains.

The origin of the name was the belief, especially widespread in France during the 1800s, that the Romany Gypsy tribe, which supposedly displayed these characteristics, came from Bohemia.

In fact, Bohemia first emerged as a political entity in the ninth century, was for a time the center of the Holy Roman Empire, and later became a kingdom in the Hapsburg Empire. Bohemia today refers to the western part of Czechoslovakia, including the capital city of Prague.

Although Bohemia is the most industrialized and urbanized area of Czechoslovakia and the people there may not have the carefree attitudes toward life that the name implies, they do have a long tradition

75

of folk culture, especially in dress, music, architecture, glasswork, and embroidery.

HUNGARY

6 tablespoons dry yeast
¼ cup plus 1 tablespoon butter or
   margarine, melted
Salt
4 cups flour
2 cups warm milk
5 egg yolks
⅓ cup sugar
1 tablespoon rum
Cooking oil
Confectioners' sugar
½ cup apricot jam
½ cup apricot brandy

Apricot Brandy Doughnuts

These doughnuts with a jam and brandy filling combine in one dish a delicious dessert and an after-dinner drink.

1. Combine yeast, 1 tablespoon of the butter, dash of salt, and ½ cup of the flour, mixing together well. Stir in ½ cup of the milk. Let sit in a warm place for 20 to 25 minutes to rise.

2. Combine risen dough, remaining 3½ cups flour, remaining 1½ cups milk, egg yolks, sugar, and dash of salt. Gradually add rum and remaining ¼ cup of butter. Knead until dough becomes fairly stiff and smooth. Cover with a cloth and let sit in a warm place for about 1 hour to rise.

3. Roll out dough on a floured surface to a thickness of 1½ to 2 inches. Cut into circles about 3½ inches in diameter. Let sit in a warm place for about 30 minutes to rise.

4. Heat oil to very hot. Press middle of doughnut to assure thorough cooking and to form a well for the jam. Gently place doughnuts, one

at a time, into hot oil and fry until golden brown. Remove from oil and drain on paper towels. Sprinkle with confectioners' sugar.

5. Mix together apricot jam and apricot brandy and spoon into center well of doughnuts.

Yield: approximately 1 dozen doughnuts

HUNGARY □ Hungarian goulash is really a soup, not a stew, as most people outside Hungary believe it to be.

The traditional ingredients are cubes of beef or other meat, onions, potatoes, green peppers, tomatoes, small dumplings, gravy, and a liberal amount of paprika, the spice that is used in many Hungarian dishes.

LITHUANIA

3 cups mixed berries and chopped
   fruits (raspberries, strawberries,
   cranberries, cherries, plums)
3 cups cold water
Sugar
1 teaspoon cornstarch mixed with
   1 tablespoon water
Cream or milk

Fruit Pudding

Winters in Lithuania along the Baltic Sea can sometimes be harsh, but they are much easier to bear knowing that this fruit pudding is always available.

1. Combine berries and chopped fruits with the water in a heavy saucepan and heat to boiling. Continue boiling until berries and fruit are soft.

2. Remove from heat, pour into a blender, and purée. Measure

purée, return to saucepan, place over medium heat, and add 1 tea-spoon sugar for every cup of purée, mixing well. Stir in cornstarch and water mixture. Heat to boiling, stirring constantly, and then boil for about 5 minutes.

3. Pour into individual serving bowls that have been rinsed in cold water. Chill in refrigerator and serve with cream and milk.

Yield: 6 servings

LITHUANIA □ Lithuanian folk songs are especially appealing because the language has many diminutives and endearing forms of both nouns and adjectives, which instantly express strong emotional feelings.

The language of Lithuania also has many onomatopoeic formations —words that sound like what they mean *(whoops, buzz, ouch)*. Another characteristic of Lithuanian is that new words are continually created, so it is just about impossible to have a dictionary containing all the words of the language.

POLAND

¾ cup sugar
½ cup boiling water
4 egg yolks, beaten
1 teaspoon vanilla extract
½ cup milk
1½ tablespoons (1½ envelopes, ¼
ounce each) unflavored gelatin
softened in 3 tablespoons boiling
water
1 cup heavy cream, whipped
2 egg whites, stiffly beaten

Caramel Cream

It may be difficult to define "old-world charm" but after having this caramel cream from Poland you will know that this dessert is part of it.

1. Place ¼ cup sugar in a saucepan over medium-high heat until it turns dark golden brown. Add boiling water and stir until sugar dissolves. Remove from heat and set aside to cool completely.

2. Cream together in a heavy saucepan remaining ½ cup sugar, egg yolks, and vanilla and heat over boiling water. Add milk and beat well. Add dissolved sugar and softened gelatin, mixing until it becomes very thick. Mix in heavy cream and egg whites. Remove from heat.

3. Spoon pudding into individual serving dishes and let stand until set. Prepare several hours before serving.

Yield: 4 to 6 servings

POLAND □ Two Polish military heroes have very close ties to the Revolutionary War fought by the American colonists.

Casimir Pulaski was born in 1748 in the city of Warka, about thirty-five miles from Warsaw. He was forced to flee Poland after leading an unsuccessful revolt against Russia and wound up in France. There he met Benjamin Franklin who told him about the American struggle. Pulaski arrived in America in 1777 and organized a cavalry and light infantry corps that became known as Pulaski's Legion. He was fatally wounded while leading his troops during the siege of Savannah, Georgia. The beautiful seventeenth-century manor house in which he was born is now the Pulaski Museum.

Thaddeus Kosciusko was a brigadier general in the Colonial Army, building many fortifications in New York State, including those at West Point. After the Revolutionary War, he returned to Poland and led the Kosciusko Uprising in 1794 against Russia, Prussia, and Austria. He is buried in the historic Wawel Castle in Krakow, the burial place of many Polish heroes.

SOVIET UNION

3 tablespoons heavy cream
8 ounces creamed cottage cheese
½ cup butter or margarine, softened
3 hard-boiled egg yolks
3 tablespoons sugar
1 teaspoon vanilla extract
¼ cup candied fruit
¼ cup raisins

Candied Fruit Cottage Cheese

This cheese dessert is delicious by itself, or it can be served as a festive topping for angel food cake or poundcake.

1. Beat together heavy cream, cottage cheese, butter, egg yolks, and sugar until smooth. Add vanilla, candied fruit, and raisins.
2. Pour mixture into a 1-quart mold lined with cheesecloth that has been wrung out in cold water.
3. Chill in refrigerator for at least 6 hours. Remove from mold and serve.
Yield: 6 to 8 servings

SOVIET UNION □ The Kremlin in Moscow is generally thought of as being just the seat of the Soviet government but, in fact, it is a massive fortress enclosed by twelve-foot thick walls nearly five hundred years old.

In addition to housing the meeting chambers of the Supreme Soviet parliament, government offices, and ceremonial reception halls, the Kremlin includes within its walls numerous cathedrals, palaces, guard towers, a bell tower, the czar's imperial family apartments, and the czar's crown jewels.

81

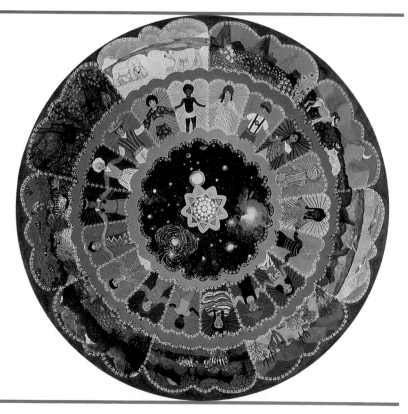

The Earth is but One Country, by Jill Rosenberg,
United States of America. UNICEF card issued in
1978.

Happy Town, appliqué by Birte Bjaerris, Denmark. UNICEF card issued in 1977.

Sailing, by Olga Troconis, Colombia.
UNICEF card issued in 1982.

Carrousel, by José Ramón Śánchez, Spain. UNICEF card issued in 1983.

THE BALKANS

BULGARIA

1 cup orange marmalade
1 cup water
1 cup chopped walnuts
2 cups confectioners' sugar
½ cup raisins
1 teaspoon baking soda
1 teaspoon ground cinnamon
¼ teaspoon grated lemon peel
4 cups flour
Sugar Syrup (recipe follows)

SUGAR SYRUP
½ cup sugar
1 cup water

Marmalade and Walnut Cake

The orange marmalade makes this cake especially moist and also gives it a distinctive taste.

1. Preheat oven to 350° F.
2. Mix together marmalade and water. Add walnuts, sugar, raisins, baking soda, cinnamon, lemon peel, and flour, mixing well.
3. Spread batter in a 9x13-inch greased baking pan. Bake at 350° F for 40 to 50 minutes, until cake tests clean.
4. Remove from oven, poke holes in top of cake with a toothpick, and pour warm Sugar Syrup over warm cake.
Yield: 10 to 12 servings

Combine sugar and water in a saucepan and heat until sugar dissolves and mixture comes to a full boil.

BULGARIA □ The Bulgarian renaissance from 1830 to 1880 was that country's greatest cultural movement of modern times.

In addition to producing notable works by writers, poets, and artists, it was also a time of significant architectural achievement. Woodcarvings were made, murals and icons were painted, and new textile products in embroidery and tapestries were created. Since it was also an era of economic prosperity and new religious freedom, many public buildings, private homes and businesses, and churches were renovated, constructed, and decorated.

The accomplishments of this period can still be seen in the older sections of many Bulgarian cities, especially Plovdiv, Koprivshtitsa, Turnovo, Tryavna, and Samokov.

GREECE

6 cups chopped walnuts
5 cups coarsely broken up zwieback toast
½ cup sugar
3 tablespoons ground cinnamon
12 strudel dough leaves, each 9 x 13 inches
1 cup butter or margarine, melted
Honey and Sugar Syrup (recipe follows)

Baklava

Here is one of those rare desserts that appeals to your ears as well as to your eyes and mouth. The sizzling sound that the hot syrup makes when you pour it over the cinnamon and nut pastry as it comes out of the oven will become one of the favorite sounds in your kitchen.

1. Preheat oven to 350° F.
2. Mix together walnuts, zwieback, sugar, and cinnamon in a large bowl. Divide mixture into three equal parts. Set aside.
3. Place 1 strudel dough leaf on the bottom of a 9x13-inch pan and brush it with melted butter. Place another strudel dough leaf on top and again brush with melted butter. Repeat with 2 more strudel dough leaves.
4. Evenly spread one third of walnut mixture over strudel dough

leaves in pan. Cover with 2 more strudel dough leaves, brushing each one with melted butter. Evenly spread another third of the walnut mixture over strudel dough leaves in pan and cover with 2 more buttered strudel dough leaves. Spread remaining walnut mixture evenly over strudel dough leaves in pan and cover with remaining 4 strudel dough leaves, brushing each leaf with melted butter as it is placed in the pan.

5. Using a serrated knife and a sawing motion, cut pastry lengthwise in pan three times, making 4 equal strips, each about 2 inches wide. Cut strips diagonally at 2-inch intervals, making diamond-shaped pieces.

6. Bake at 350° F for 30 to 40 minutes, until golden brown. Remove from oven and immediately pour hot Honey and Sugar Syrup slowly and evenly over pastry.

Yield: approximately 2½ dozen pastries

HONEY AND SUGAR SYRUP
2 cups sugar
2½ cups water
2 cinnamon sticks
½ cup honey
½ teaspoon lemon juice

1. Combine sugar and water in a saucepan and cook over medium heat, stirring constantly, until sugar dissolves. Add cinnamon sticks and increase heat until mixture comes to a rapid boil.

2. Reduce heat and let simmer for 20 minutes. Add honey and simmer for several minutes longer, until pastry is done.

3. Remove from heat, discard cinnamon sticks, and add lemon juice.

GREECE □ The Greek people have a legend explaining why their country has so many rocks and why there are so many mountains.

As they tell it, when God created the world He sifted the earth through a strainer to remove most of the rocks and stones. God then threw away all the rocks and stones that were left in the strainer and they all happened to land in Greece.

ROMANIA

Lemon Soufflé

6 egg yolks, beaten
½ cup sugar
½ cup butter or margarine, melted
3 teaspoons lemon juice
Dash salt
½ teaspoon grated lemon peel
6 egg whites, beaten until fluffy

Light and airy with a delicate lemon flavor, this soufflé is the perfect ending to a heavy meal.

1. Combine egg yolks and sugar in a heavy pan and heat over hot water. Slowly add butter. Add lemon juice, salt, and lemon peel, stirring constantly. Remove from heat and let cool.
2. Preheat oven to 325° F.
3. Fold in egg whites. Spoon mixture into a greased 1½-quart ovenware dish and place dish in a pan of hot water. Bake at 325° F for about 45 minutes, until golden brown.

Yield: 4 servings

ROMANIA □ The Danube River passes through eight countries in Central Europe and then flows into the Black Sea. Although it was the section of the river near the Vienna Woods that inspired Johann Strauss's immortal waltz, *Blue Danube*, the most noteworthy part of the Danube today is its delta in northeastern Romania.

The Danube Delta covers an area larger than the state of Rhode Island, and millions of scientists, nature lovers, and tourists come to Romania each year to study and enjoy the many different kinds of wildlife and vegetation in this area of marshes, lagoons, islands, lakes, sand bars, and reed beds.

TURKEY

1 cup cold water
4 tablespoons cornstarch
2 grapefruits
1 large orange
2 cups orange juice
2 cups grapefruit juice
1½ cups sugar
1 cup chopped blanched almonds
1 cup pomegranate seeds, if desired
1 cup whipped cream

Grapefruit and Orange Pudding

If you want a nice combination of fruits and nuts, look no further than this Turkish delight of citrus fruits and almonds.

1. Combine water and cornstarch, stirring well. Set aside.
2. Peel grapefruits and orange and cut into segments. Remove seeds and membranes. Set aside.
3. Combine orange and grapefruit juices and sugar in a saucepan. Stir cornstarch mixture again and add to juices in saucepan.
4. Cook juice mixture over medium heat, stirring constantly, for about 20 minutes, until pudding thickens and begins to bubble. Add orange and grapefruit segments and cook for 2 minutes more, stirring gently. Remove from heat and stir in almonds.
5. Spoon pudding into individual serving dishes and chill in refrigerator for at least 3 hours. Decorate with pomegranate seeds, if desired, and serve with whipped cream.

Yield: 6 to 8 servings

TURKEY □ Istanbul, the largest city in Turkey, is divided in two by the Bosporus Strait, with part of the city in Europe and the other part in Asia.

The Bosporus Bridge that connects the two sections of Istanbul is

89

the longest bridge in Asia and continental Europe, and the only bridge in the world that connects two continents.

YUGOSLAVIA

1 cup milk
1 can (12½ ounces) poppy filling
2 apples
1 cup confectioners' sugar
2 teaspoons vanilla extract
½ cup heavy cream
½ cup peach preserves
2 cups raisins
6 strudel dough leaves, each 9 x 13 inches
¾ cup unsalted butter or margarine, melted
1 small egg, beaten, mixed with 2 teaspoons milk

Poppy Fruit Strudel

Poppy filling is used in a variety of pastries but you will have a hard time finding any poppy dessert that is more delicious than this strudel.

1. Preheat oven to 375° F.
2. Place milk in a heavy saucepan and heat to boiling. Reduce heat, add poppy filling, and cook for 5 minutes more. Remove from heat and set aside to cool.
3. Peel and core apples and cut into small pieces. Add apples, sugar, vanilla, cream, peach preserves, and raisins to poppy mixture, stirring well. Set aside.
4. Brush each strudel leaf with melted butter and stack one on top of another on cheesecloth or a towel. Spoon poppy mixture along one long edge of strudel leaves. Roll strudel dough around filling.
5. Brush egg and milk mixture over top of strudel roll.
6. Bake at 375° F for about 45 minutes, until strudel is flaky and golden brown. Cut into thick slices and serve warm.

Yield: 6 to 8 servings

YUGOSLAVIA □ Even with the great popularity of radio, television, movies, and other forms of commercial entertainment, the Yugoslavian custom of *korzo* is still very much alive among people of all ages throughout the country.

Korzo is the traditional evening stroll around the town square, along the waterfront, down the main street, through the marketplace, or wherever the center of town might be, with no more urgent purpose than to socialize, chat with friends and neighbors, provide a pleasant end to the day, and, of course, to see and be seen.

AFRICA

IVORY COAST

8 mangoes, pitted, peeled, and sliced,
    or 2 cups canned mangoes, drained
    and sliced
Pie Shell (recipe follows)
½ cup sugar
1 teaspoon ground cinnamon
Dash salt
¼ teaspoon grated nutmeg
1 tablespoon flour
1 tablespoon butter
1 egg yolk, lightly beaten

PIE SHELL
2½ cups flour
1 teaspoon baking powder
½ cup sugar
1 egg, lightly beaten
½ cup milk
2 tablespoons butter or margarine,
    softened

Mango Pie

This mango filling in a sweet cookie-like crust will be a welcome change from the usual apple, cherry, and blueberry pies.

1. Preheat oven to 425° F.
2. Place mangoes evenly in unbaked Pie Shell. Sprinkle with sugar, cinnamon, salt, nutmeg, and flour. Dot with butter.
3. Place strips of dough from Pie Shell across top in a lattice pattern. Brush with egg yolk.
4. Bake at 425° F for about 30 minutes, until crust is golden brown.
Yield: 8 to 10 servings

1. Mix together flour, baking powder, and sugar. Combine egg and milk and add to dough. Add butter and knead until dough can be rolled out.
2. Roll out dough to ¼-inch thickness and line a 9-inch pie pan. Shape excess dough into 6 strips, each strip 9 inches long, for top of pie.

IVORY COAST □ Wood carving is one of the most widespread and important folk arts in the Ivory Coast, and the country is a major center

94

for this craft in Africa. There is an outstanding collection in the Ifan Museum in the capital city of Abidjan.

Most of the wood carvings are made by Baoulé craftsmen and their homes are frequently decorated with examples of their work, including beautifully carved doors, furniture, and statues.

MAURITIUS

1 can (20 ounces) crushed pineapple
1 cup water
1 cup sugar
2 tablespoons (two envelopes, ¼ ounce each) unflavored gelatin dissolved in ½ cup water
2 egg whites, stiffly beaten
Custard Cream (recipe follows)

Pineapple Bombe

The only thing militant about this bombe is how good you will feel about serving and eating this delicious combination of pineapple and custard.

1. Combine pineapple, water, and sugar in a heavy pan and boil for 5 minutes, stirring occasionally. Remove from heat.
2. Add dissolved gelatin, mixing well. Fold in egg whites.
3. Pour mixture into a wet 1½-quart mold and chill in refrigerator.
4. Remove from mold and pour Custard Cream over top.
Yield: 4 to 6 servings

(continued)

CUSTARD CREAM

2 egg yolks
1 teaspoon cornstarch
2 tablespoons sugar
1 tablespoon vanilla extract
2 cups milk

1. Combine egg yolks, cornstarch, and sugar, mixing together until smooth and creamy. Set aside.
2. Add vanilla to milk and heat to a boil.
3. Pour milk mixture into egg yolk mixture, beating continuously. Cook over low heat until custard comes to a boil.
4. Remove from heat and chill in refrigerator.

MAURITIUS ☐ Bernardin de Saint-Pierre was a French author who lived from 1737 to 1814 and was greatly influenced by the naturalistic philosophy of his close friend Jean-Jacques Rousseau.

His most famous work, the short novel *Paul et Virginie*, is set on the island of Mauritius in the Indian Ocean off the southeast coast of Africa. Bernardin had been stationed on Mauritius in 1768 as an engineer in the French Army, and he drew upon his experiences there to create the tropical paradise setting for his tale of man's nobility in a natural environment. The story is as well known for its descriptions of the tropical surroundings as it is for its tragic love story.

MOROCCO

Sesame Cookies

1 cup ground sesame seeds
2 cups oil
1 cup ground almonds
3 eggs, beaten
1½ cups sugar
1 teaspoon vanilla extract
1 teaspoon ground cinnamon
1 teaspoon rose flower water
4 cups flour
2 tablespoons baking powder

The North African coast may be thousands of miles away, but the distinctive almond and sesame seed flavor of these small, crisp cookies will bring that part of the world closer to you.

1. Preheat oven to 375° F.
2. Mix together well sesame seeds, oil, almonds, eggs, sugar, vanilla, cinnamon, and rose flower water. Sift together flour and baking powder and gradually add to mixture. Knead well.
3. Shape dough into 1-inch balls and place on a greased cookie sheet. Bake at 375° F for 12 to 15 minutes.

Yield: approximately 10 dozen cookies

MOROCCO □ The name Casablanca evokes images of wartime intrigues, slowly turning ceiling fans, mist-shrouded airports, and a piano player singing "As Time Goes By."

However true that picture might have been forty years ago, Casablanca today is an important commercial and industrial center with nearly two million people. It is the largest city and chief port of Morocco and boasts broad boulevards, large skyscrapers, luxury hotels, and attractive office buildings, many of them built in the modern style of the renowned French architect Le Corbusier.

SEYCHELLES

6 large bananas, sliced
2 tablespoons sugar
3 tablespoons butter or margarine,
   melted
1 teaspoon ground cinnamon
1 cup rum

Bananas Flambé

This dessert will light up your meal, not only with its great taste but also with a spectacular flaming entrance that everyone will remember for a long time.

1. Preheat oven to 425° F.
2. Place banana slices in a 3-quart ovenware dish and sprinkle 1 tablespoon of the sugar over top. Add butter and mix together well.
3. Bake at 425° F for 20 minutes.
4. Remove from oven and sprinkle cinnamon and remaining tablespoon of sugar over top. Pour rum over bananas and ignite. Serve flaming.

Yield: 4 servings

SEYCHELLES □ The ninety-two islands and islets that make up the Seychelles have a total land area of only 108 square miles—smaller than the city of Charlotte, North Carolina. They are scattered over four hundred thousand square miles of the Indian Ocean one thousand miles off the east coast of Africa.

Although the nation of Seychelles may be small, its bird population is large and includes many of the rarest birds on earth, like the black parrot and the paradise flycatcher. Some of the islands have been designated as bird sanctuaries and ornithologists and other scientists come from all over the world for research and study.

<hr>

SOUTH AFRICA

1½ cups flour
4 teaspoons baking powder
½ teaspoon salt
2 tablespoons butter or margarine, softened
½ cup buttermilk, or ½ cup milk mixed with ½ tablespoon vinegar
Cooking oil
Syrup (recipe follows)

Braids

These braided pastry cookies are just the right touch when you want an attractive and tasty dessert that is not too sweet.

1. Sift together flour, baking powder, and salt. Add butter and buttermilk, kneading well. Let dough stand for 15 minutes.
2. Roll out dough to ¼-inch thickness and cut into strips ¼ inch wide by 3 inches long. Braid in groups of three, firmly pressing together the ends of the strips.
3. Heat the oil to very hot and fry the braids until golden brown. Drain, dip into ice-cold Syrup, and let dry on a wire rack.
    Yield: approximately 3½ dozen braids

(continued)

SYRUP

¼ teaspoon grated lemon peel
Juice of 1 lemon
4½ cups sugar
2 cups water
½ teaspoon ground ginger
¼ teaspoon cream of tartar
Dash salt

Combine lemon peel, lemon juice, sugar, water, ginger, cream of tartar, and salt in a saucepan and stir until sugar dissolves. Simmer for 3 to 5 minutes, remove from heat, and chill thoroughly in freezer.

SOUTH AFRICA □ After a young girl found a diamond while playing in a field near Kimberley, South Africa, in 1867, five diamond mines began operations there and the city became known as the "Diamond Capital of the World."

Four of the five are still worked today; the fifth, the Kimberley Mine, ceased operations in 1915 after yielding over 14 million carats of diamonds. The unused mine has been preserved as a huge open-air museum with the largest excavation ever made by man, a hole one-third of a mile wide and one-quarter of a mile deep.

SUDAN

8 oranges
1½ cups sugar
1 cup water
¼ cup brandy
2 tablespoons Grand Marnier or
Cointreau
Whipped Cream, if desired

Brandied Oranges

Here is a new way to enjoy oranges: a tasty sauce that can be eaten by itself or served over cakes, waffles, ice cream or anything else for a sophisticated new dish.

1. Cut oranges in half and, working over a large bowl to catch any juice, remove individual segments of the oranges between the membrane; place segments in the bowl. Squeeze juice from remaining orange peels into bowl and remove any seeds or pieces of membrane. Set aside.
2. Combine sugar and water in a heavy pan and cook over low heat, stirring constantly, until sugar dissolves. Bring to a boil and boil for 2 minutes. Let cool and mix in brandy and Grand Marnier.
3. Pour brandy mixture over orange segments. Let oranges stand for 24 hours in sauce to absorb flavors.
4. Serve topped with whipped cream, if desired.
Yield: 4 servings

SUDAN □ Visitors to the Red Sea coast of the Sudan are able to enjoy a special attraction in addition to the delightful swimming, sailing, fishing, and sightseeing trips on glass-bottom boats to view coral formations and marine life.

101

When Port Sudan became the country's main port on the Red Sea around the turn of the century, the old city of Suakin, about thirty miles down the coast, was gradually abandoned. Although the buildings in the deserted city are now crumbling, there are still many beautiful houses to be seen there, including some that are masterpieces of Islamic art.

TANZANIA

¾ cup flour
1 teaspoon baking powder
3 tablespoons butter or margarine,
  softened
¼ cup sugar
1½ cups flaked coconut
1 small egg, beaten
¼ cup milk

Coconut Cookies

The traditional foods of Tanzania include very few desserts but, fortunately, this light cookie with a delicious coconut flavor is one of them.

1. Preheat oven to 350° F.
2. Sift together flour and baking powder. Knead in butter. Add sugar and ¾ cup of the coconut, mixing well. Mix in egg and milk.
3. Using lightly greased hands, shape mixture into 1½-inch balls. Roll balls in remaining ¾ cup of coconut.
4. Place on a greased cookie sheet about 2 inches apart and bake at 350° F for 15 minutes.

Yield: approximately 20 cookies

TANZANIA □ Kilimanjaro, the highest mountain in Africa, lies in northeastern Tanzania and was immortalized in Ernest Hemingway's story *The Snows of Kilimanjaro* and the motion-picture adaptation starring Susan Hayward, Ava Gardner, and Gregory Peck.

Although the mountain is justly notable for its height, Kilimanjaro's great bulk is perhaps even more impressive. At the altitude of 16,000 feet, the mountain still covers an area of more than 40 square miles.

TUNISIA

Pistachio Stuffed Dates

1 cup crushed pistachios
1 teaspoon sugar
½ teaspoon rose flower water
½ teaspoon water
32 dates
Sugar Syrup (recipe follows)
Sugar

This date and nut candy is a welcome change from what is usually available.

1. Mix together well pistachios, 1 teaspoon sugar, rose flower water, and water.
2. Cut dates lengthwise, remove pits, and fill with pistachio paste.
3. Dip stuffed dates in Sugar Syrup and roll in sugar. Let dry overnight.

Yield: 32 stuffed dates

(continued)

SUGAR SYRUP
1 cup water
½ cup sugar

Combine water and sugar and heat to boiling, stirring constantly until sugar dissolves and mixture thickens.

TUNISIA □ The Hammamet area along the Mediterranean coast of Tunisia has become an elegant resort attracting visitors seeking the same pleasures of sun, sea, and society offered by the French Riviera.

The great French musician George Sebastian had a villa in Hammamet, a building so striking in design that Frank Lloyd Wright called it the "most beautiful house I know." The Tunisian government bought the villa about twenty-five years ago and it is now part of the International Cultural Center in Hammamet.

THE MIDDLE EAST

EGYPT

1½ cups unsalted butter or
    margarine, melted
4 cups farina
1¼ cups warm milk
1 cup flaked coconut
4 cups sugar
1 teaspoon baking powder
Slivered almonds
2 cups water
2 teaspoons lemon juice

Farina Squares

Farina is much more than just a breakfast cereal as you will find out from these marvelously rich cake squares.

1. Stir butter into farina. Add milk, coconut, 1 cup of the sugar, and baking powder, mixing together well.
2. Spread mixture evenly in a 9x13-inch baking dish, cut into 2-inch squares, and top each square with slivered almonds. Let stand for 30 minutes.
3. Preheat oven to 350° F.
4. Combine remaining 3 cups of sugar and water in a heavy saucepan and cook over medium heat, stirring constantly, until sugar dissolves and mixture comes to a boil. Add lemon juice and boil 1 minute longer. Set aside to cool.
5. Bake farina squares at 350° F for about 45 minutes, until golden brown. Remove from oven and pour cooled sugar mixture over top. Let cool.

Yield: approximately 2 dozen squares

EGYPT □ One of the greatest archaeological rescue operations of all time took place in Egypt during the late 1960s.

The Temple of Abu Simbel stood on the western bank of the Nile

106

River nearly eight hundred miles south of Cairo. It was built over three thousand years ago by the great Pharaoh Ramses II. Because the completion of the Aswan Dam would cover the Temple with the waters of the Nile, an international rescue effort was launched through the United Nations Educational, Scientific, and Cultural Organization.

The massive temple was dismantled and the 400,000 tons of stone were crated, transported to the top of the cliff ninety feet directly above the original site, and then reassembled exactly as they were before.

Fifty nations and millions of people around the world gave both financial and technical support to this tremendous relocation project.

IRAQ

1 tablespoon dry yeast
1 teaspoon sugar
1¼ cups warm water
1½ cups flour
Orange Flower Syrup (recipe follows)

Pancakes With Orange Flower Syrup

The orange flower syrup makes these pancakes a very special treat not only for dessert but also for breakfast or lunch.

1. Dissolve yeast and sugar in ¼ cup of the water and let stand in a warm place for about 10 minutes, until mixture begins to bubble.
2. Combine yeast mixture with flour in a large bowl and then gradually add remaining cup of water, stirring until batter becomes smooth. Batter will be very loose.

3. Cover with a cloth and let stand in a warm place for about 1 hour. Batter will rise and become bubbly and slightly elastic.

4. Spoon batter by tablespoonfuls onto a lightly greased hot pan and cook over medium heat until pancake becomes bubbly and separates from pan easily. Turn pancake over and cook for another minute or two.

5. Remove from pan and serve with cold Orange Flower Syrup.

Yield: approximately 3 dozen pancakes.

ORANGE FLOWER SYRUP

2½ cups sugar
1¼ cups water
1 tablespoon lemon juice
2 tablespoons orange flower water

1. Combine sugar, water, and lemon juice in a heavy saucepan and cook over medium heat, stirring constantly, until sugar dissolves and mixture comes to a boil. Let simmer for 3 to 4 minutes without stirring. Stir in orange flower water and simmer for another 2 minutes.

2. Remove from heat, let cool, and then chill in refrigerator.

IRAQ □ The history of human settlement in Iraq goes back thousands of years and includes some of the oldest civilizations on earth. There were the Sumerians with their cities of Ur and Uruk; King Hammurabi and his capital of Babylon; the great Assyrian cities of Nineveh, Nimrud and Ashur; and King Nebuchadnezzar, who built the famed Hanging Gardens of Babylon, one of the Seven Wonders of the World.

In addition to these early peoples, the greatest ancient settlement of all was also in Iraq. The Tigris and Euphrates rivers join together at Al Qurnah in southeastern Iraq, which was, according to the Bible, the location of the Garden of Eden.

108

ISRAEL

3½ cups flour
Dash salt
1½ teaspoons baking powder
1 teaspoon baking soda
½ teaspoon ground cinnamon
¼ teaspoon ground nutmeg
⅛ teaspoon ground cloves
¼ teaspoon ground ginger
¾ cup sugar
4 eggs, beaten
¼ cup vegetable oil
2 cups honey
½ cup brewed coffee
1½ cups chopped walnuts or
*   almonds*

Honey Cake

Israel is known as the "Land of Milk and Honey" and the sweetness of this honey cake is a traditional New Year's symbol of best wishes for the coming twelve months.

1. Preheat oven to 325° F.
2. Sift together flour, salt, baking powder, baking soda, cinnamon, nutmeg, cloves, and ginger. Set aside.
3. Gradually add sugar to eggs and beat until mixture is thick and light in color. Beat in oil, honey, and coffee. Stir in flour mixture and nuts.
4. Spoon batter into two 9-inch loaf pans that have been greased and lined with wax paper or aluminum foil. Bake at 325° F for 1¼ to 1½ hours, until cake tests clean with toothpick.
5. Cool on cake rack and then remove from pan.
Yield: 20 to 24 servings

ISRAEL □ Jaffa, right next to Tel Aviv, is one of the oldest cities in the world and it has been the site of many ancient adventures. According to the Roman historian Plinius, Jaffa gets its name from Japhet, the third son of Noah, who founded the city forty years after the Great Flood.

109

Jonah set sail from Jaffa on his voyage that ended in the belly of a whale, and in Greek mythology Perseus rescued Andromeda from a rock in Jaffa harbor, where she had been chained as a sacrifice to a sea monster. Cedars from Lebanon were unloaded in Jaffa by King Solomon for building his temple in Jerusalem, and the Jewish Maccabees, the heroes of the holiday of Hanukkah, occupied the city in the 2nd century B.C.

JORDAN

1 cup coarsely chopped pistachios
¼ teaspoon sugar
2 drops orange flower water
12 strudel dough leaves, each 9x13 inches
½ cup butter or margarine, melted
Syrup (recipe follows)

Pistachio Pastry Rings

In Jordan these pistachio pastries are called "Princess Bracelets" and they are, indeed, a dessert good enough to be served to royalty.

1. Preheat oven to 350° F.
2. Combine chopped pistachios, sugar, and orange flower water, mixing well. Set aside.
3. Cut strudel dough leaves in half so leaves now measure 9 inches by 6½ inches. Working with 12 of the strudel dough leaves, tightly roll up each leaf along the long edge, forming a tube-like roll, and then bend each roll into a ring and crimp the two ends together.
4. Place the 12 rings on greased cookie sheets. Fold the remaining

12 strudel dough leaves into fourths. Gently press a folded leaf into the center of each ring to form a flat bed to hold the filling.

5. Brush pastries with butter and bake at 350° F for 20 minutes, until light golden brown.

6. Remove from oven, spoon pistachio mixture into center of each ring, and drizzle Syrup over pastry. Leave pastries on cookie sheets for about 1 hour before serving.

Yield: 1 dozen pastries

SYRUP
½ cup sugar
½ cup plus 2 tablespoons water
2 tablespoons honey
⅛ teaspoon ground cinnamon
½ teaspoon lemon juice

1. Combine sugar and water in a heavy saucepan and cook over medium heat, stirring constantly, until sugar dissolves. Bring to a boil, reduce heat to a simmer, and let cook for 20 minutes without stirring.

2. Remove from heat and stir in honey, cinnamon, and lemon juice.

JORDAN □ Jordan sits at the crossroads of the Middle East, and empires and armies have swept back and forth across its land for thousands of years.

It is not surprising that a wealth of archaeological ruins have been found in Jordan, including a Roman theater in downtown Amman; the Greek and Roman city of Jarash; Byzantine mosaics; Crusader castles at Al Karak and Ajlun; six palaces from the Umayyad dynasty that ruled the Islamic Empire from A.D. 661 to 750; and the rock city of Petra, the capital of the Nabataeans from the 4th century B.C. to A.D. 106.

111

LEBANON

1 cup rice, finely ground
5 cups cold water
1 cup sugar
1 teaspoon or ½ teaspoon powdered
   anise seed
1 teaspoon fennel seeds, or ½
   teaspoon powdered fennel seeds
1 teaspoon caraway seeds, or ½
   teaspoon powdered caraway seeds
2 teaspoons ground cinnamon
½ cup slivered almonds

Festive Rice Pudding

For those of you who like rice pudding but are tired of eating the same thing time after time, here is a nice change with a truly different taste because of the out-of-the-ordinary spices that are used.

1. Combine rice and 2½ cups of the water, mixing together well. Add sugar, anise seed, fennel seed, caraway seed, and cinnamon. Set aside.
2. Heat remaining 2½ cups water to boiling, gradually add rice mixture, stirring vigorously with a wooden spoon. Continue stirring until mixture returns to a boil. Lower heat and simmer, stirring often, for about 30 minutes, until mixture coats spoon.
3. Remove from heat, let cool, and spoon into individual serving dishes. Sprinkle almonds over top and chill in refrigerator.
   Yield: 8 to 10 servings

LEBANON □ There are many different types of cedar trees around the world, but best known of all are the legendary Cedars of Lebanon.

They were used by the Phoenicians to build their merchant ships, which traded throughout the ancient world, and King Solomon used these trees in the construction of his temple in Jerusalem.

Most of the cedar trees now growing in Lebanon are comparatively recent replants, but high in the mountains above Tripoli in northern Lebanon stands a forest of the ancient Cedars of Lebanon with many trees dating back more than one thousand years.

SAUDI ARABIA

18 walnut halves
18 figs, cut lengthwise almost in half
½ lemon
¼ cup sugar
2 tablespoons honey
1 clove
½ cup plain yogurt
¼ teaspoon vanilla extract

Figs in Syrup

When you start to eat these figs in syrup, close your eyes, let your imagination wander, and soon you will find yourself resting in the sand at a desert oasis, enjoying the welcome shade while your camel patiently waits nearby to resume the journey.

1. Place 1 walnut half into each cut fig and press sides of fig together. Set aside.

2. Using a vegetable peeler, cut a thin 2-inch long strip of lemon peel. Set aside.

3. Squeeze juice from the lemon half into a measuring cup and add enough water to measure ½ cup.

4. Combine in a heavy saucepan lemon peel strip, lemon juice mixed with water, sugar, honey, and clove. Heat to boiling, reduce heat, and continue to cook, stirring frequently, until syrup becomes thick and bubbly.

5. Remove from heat, discard lemon peel and clove, and let cool slightly. Mix in yogurt and vanilla.

6. Pour syrup over figs, cover, and chill in the refrigerator.
Yield: 18 stuffed figs

SAUDI ARABIA □ Two of the holiest sites of Islam are located in the cities of Mecca and Medina in Saudi Arabia.

The Kaaba, the small cubic building in the Great Mosque in Mecca, houses the Black Stone, the most sacred Muslim object. One of the essential duties in Islam is to make a pilgrimage to the Kaaba in Mecca.

Muhammad used the city of Medina as his base for converting and conquering Arabia. The large mosque in Medina contains the tombs of Muhammad and his daughter Fatima.

SYRIA

2¼ cups flour
1 cup shortening, melted
¼ teaspoon dry yeast dissolved in
  ½ cup water
½ cup crushed pistachios
½ teaspoon confectioners' sugar
1 teaspoon orange flower water
½ teaspoon water
Confectioners' sugar

Pistachio Cookies

Each time you bite into the pistachio filling in the enclosed center of one of these cookies it is like unwrapping another present.

1. Combine flour and shortening and knead by hand for 20 minutes, gradually adding dissolved yeast. Cover and let rest 1½ hours.
2. Mix together pistachios and ½ teaspoon confectioners' sugar. Add orange flower water, blending well. Set aside.
3. Preheat oven to 350° F.
4. Working with a small handful of dough at a time, squeeze it for about 2 minutes to make it soft. Shape into a ball, and using your finger, make a hole in the center with the sides as thin as possible.
5. Fill center with pistachio mixture, close up hole, and flatten.
6. Place on a lightly greased cookie sheet and bake at 350° F for about 30 minutes. Sprinkle with confectioners' sugar. Store in a glass jar at room temperature.

Yield: approximately 3½ dozen cookies

SYRIA □ Several villages in Syria share a historical uniqueness that is not duplicated in any other country.

The ancient Semitic language of Aramaic was used throughout the Middle East from about 1000 B.C. to about A.D. 700. Jesus Christ spoke

115

it and some of the Dead Sea Scrolls, the oldest known manuscripts of the Bible, were written in Aramaic.

Aramaic was replaced by Arabic a long time ago except in a small group of villages north of Damascus where this ancient language is still spoken.

ASIA

INDIA

¼ cup butter or margarine
2 tablespoons honey
1 tablespoon lime juice
16 maraschino cherries
2 peaches, peeled, pitted, and cut into
   quarters
8 pineapple chunks
1 banana, cut into four thick slices
8 honeydew or cantaloupe balls

Fruit Kebabs

A unique and interesting combination of flavors makes these kebabs quite a change from most fruit desserts.

1. Combine butter, honey, and lime juice in a saucepan and cook over low heat, stirring occasionally, until syrup comes to a boil. Boil for about 1 minute. Remove from heat and set aside.

2. Arrange fruit pieces on 4 skewers and brush completely with honey syrup.

3. Place under broiler about 4 inches from heat and broil for 3 to 5 minutes, turning once or twice and brushing with honey syrup. Serve immediately.

Yield: 4 servings

INDIA □ Standing on the bank of the Yamuna River at Agra, the Taj Mahal is one of the finest examples of Muslim architecture in all the world. The white marble structure was built in the mid-1600s by the Mughul Emperor Shah Jahan as a mausoleum for his favorite wife, Arjumand Banu Begum, who had died while giving birth to her fourteenth child.

The building's name comes from the title given to Banu by her husband: *Mumtaz Mahal*, which means "Chosen of the Palace." Shah Jahan planned to build a replica of the Taj Mahal in black marble on the opposite bank of the Yamuna River for his own burial, but he was deposed by one of his sons before he could do so.

LAOS

3 bananas
2 cups coconut milk
¼ cup plus 2 tablespoons sugar
2 tablespoons tapioca

Hot Banana and Tapioca Pudding

Here is a versatile dessert that can be eaten by itself or used as a topping on cakes, pies, and other puddings.

1. Cut bananas into small pieces. Combine banana pieces, 1¾ cups of the coconut milk, and sugar in a heavy saucepan and cook over medium heat, while stirring, until mixture comes to a boil. Add tapioca and boil gently for about 20 minutes.
2. Remove from heat and stir in remaining ¼ cup of coconut milk. Serve hot.

Yield: 4 to 6 servings

LAOS □ Laos was given its name by the French when they took control of the country in the 1890s. It was named after the Lao Loum people who lived there.

119

Before the arrival of the French, the country was called *Lane Xang*, "the Land of a Million Elephants," because there were so many of these magnificent animals in the region.

MALAYSIA

1 cup boiling milk
⅓ cup sugar
3 egg yolks
2 tablespoons (two envelopes, ¼ ounce each) unflavored gelatin softened in 3 tablespoons boiling water
7 pineapple rings
2 tablespoons orange liqueur
1 cup heavy cream
4 slices poundcake
4 candied cherries

Pineapple Cream Cake

Some people might think that poundcake is rather plain and ordinary, but when you cover it with this pineapple cream sauce, everyone will agree that it becomes something special.

1. Combine milk, sugar, and egg yolks and cook over low heat, stirring constantly, until sugar dissolves. Mix in softened gelatin.
2. Remove from heat and chill in refrigerator until set.
3. Cut 3 of the pineapple rings into pieces. Beat chilled mixture and blend in pineapple pieces, orange liqueur, and heavy cream.
4. Place slices of poundcake on individual serving dishes, spoon pudding over top, and decorate each portion with a pineapple ring and a candied cherry.
Yield: 4 servings

MALAYSIA □ Some of the nicest crafts in Malaysia are batik-dyed fabrics that can be used for many different pieces of clothing, including scarves, sarongs, and loin cloths. The best fabrics come from the state of Kelantan on the east coast of Peninsular Malaysia.

Batik is made by applying paraffin or rice paste to those areas of a piece of material that are not to be colored by dyes. A design is drawn on a fabric and after selective and repeated applications of protective coatings and immersions in various colored dyes, the final result is a beautiful pattern on the material.

NEPAL

1 egg, beaten
1 cup nonfat dry milk powder
1 cup sugar
2½ cups water
1 tablespoon rose flower water

Milk Balls in Syrup

These little milk balls puff up as they cook so they are not only in the delicately flavored rose flower water syrup but they are filled with it as well.

1. Mix together egg and dry milk powder. Shape mixture into 1-inch balls. Set aside.

2. Combine sugar and water in a heavy saucepan and cook over medium heat, stirring until sugar dissolves. Add 1 teaspoon rose flower water.

3. Gently place milk balls in syrup and increase heat until mixture comes to a slow boil. Cover and simmer for about 15 minutes without lifting lid.

4. Remove saucepan from heat, let cool, and stir in remaining rose flower water. Spoon milk balls and syrup into a serving dish and chill in refrigerator.

Yield: approximately 1 dozen balls

NEPAL □ More than 90 percent of the Kingdom of Nepal in southcentral Asia is covered by the Himalayas, the highest mountain range in the world.

The Everest Hotel in Nepal sits at an altitude of thirteen thousand feet and claims to be the highest hotel in the world.

The legendary capital city of Katmandu was largely isolated from the rest of the world until thirty years ago when an all-weather road was completed connecting it to India.

There are more than two thousand Hindu and Buddhist temples and shrines in the city, many dating back hundreds and hundreds of years.

PAKISTAN

½ teaspoon saffron
¼ cup plus 2 teaspoons water
4 slices bread
¼ cup plus 2 tablespoons oil
1 cup sugar
½ cup half-and-half
Chopped almonds
Chopped pistachios

Saffron Syrup Toast

The saffron flavor, the crisp outside coating, and the baked-in syrup combine to make this a special chewy toasted dessert.

1. Preheat oven to 350° F.
2. Place saffron into the 2 teaspoons of water to soak. Set aside.
3. Remove crusts from bread and cut each slice in half. Fry bread in oil over low heat, until golden brown. Remove bread from oil, drain on paper towels, and place in a 9x13-inch baking dish. Set aside.
4. Combine sugar and remaining ¼ cup of water in a heavy saucepan and cook over medium heat, stirring until sugar dissolves. Boil without stirring for about 10 minutes. Remove from heat.
5. Strain saffron from water, discard saffron, and add the water to syrup. Pour syrup over bread slices in baking dish. Heat half-and-half to boiling and pour over bread.
6. Bake at 350° F for 30 minutes. Sprinkle with almonds and pistachios and serve hot or cold.

Yield: 4 servings

PAKISTAN □ The Khyber Pass in northwestern Pakistan is one of the most famous mountain passes in the world. For much of its thirty-

123

three-mile length, the pass winds its way between high cliffs of shale and limestone.

Throughout history the Khyber Pass has had great strategic value as a major trading and invasion route through Asia. The British gained control of the area in the late 1800s and formed a special military unit, the Khyber Rifles, to patrol the pass. The activities of this unit and events in the area provided the background for a movie in 1953, *King of the Khyber Rifles*, starring Tyrone Power, Terry Moore, and Michael Rennie.

Today a highway and a railroad go through the pass and connect Pakistan and Afghanistan.

PHILIPPINES

1 cup flour
1 cup nonfat dry milk powder
½ cup butter or margarine, softened
1 cup sugar
1 egg yolk
⅓ cup evaporated milk
⅓ cup water
2½ cups flaked coconut

Macaroon Cupcakes

These macaroon cupcakes will be the nicest, chewiest, and richest cupcakes you have ever eaten.

1. Preheat oven to 350° F.
2. Sift together flour and dry milk powder. Set aside.
3. Cream butter. Add sugar and beat until fluffy. Add egg yolk and evaporated milk, beating well. Mixture will look curdled. Add flour mixture alternately with water, beating well. Stir in coconut.

124

4. Place cupcake papers in muffin tin and fill halfway with batter. Bake at 350° F for 25 to 30 minutes, until nicely browned.

Yield: approximately 2 dozen cupcakes

PHILIPPINES □ Public transportation in many cities in the Philippines is provided by "jeepneys," taxis and small buses that are brightly painted and decorated with colorful designs.

The original jeepneys were made from World War II jeeps left in the Philippines after the war. The name comes from a combination of that versatile GI vehicle and the word "jitney," meaning a small bus or automobile that carries passengers along a route for a small fee.

SINGAPORE

3 apples
Lemon juice
1 egg, beaten
⅔ cup cold water
1 cup flour
Peanut oil (enough to cover apple slices)
Sesame Seed Glaze (recipe follows)

Glazed Apples

These glazed apples are not only good to eat, but also can be a fun ending to a small dinner party. The table can be set with containers and hot plates for the batter, cooking oil, glaze, and ice water, with each guest making his or her own dessert.

1. Peel, core, and cut each apple into 8 slices. Sprinkle with lemon juice.

2. Beat together egg and water and add flour all at once, beating

vigorously, until batter is smooth. Let stand for 5 to 10 minutes.

3. Heat oil to very hot. Dip apple slices in batter and fry, 1 or 2 at a time, in the hot oil, until batter becomes golden brown.

4. Using a slotted spoon, remove apple slices from oil and immediately dip into Sesame Seed Glaze, completely coating apple slices.

5. Remove apple slices from glaze and immediately immerse in a bowl of ice water. Almost at once glaze will harden and become brittle. Quickly lift apple slices from ice water and immediately serve on a lightly oiled plate. Glaze will melt and the coating will become soft if allowed to stand.

Yield: 2 dozen glazed apple slices

SESAME SEED GLAZE
1½ cups sugar
½ cup cold water
2 teaspoons sesame seeds (preferably
black sesame seeds)

Combine sugar and water in a heavy saucepan and cook over medium heat, without stirring, until mixture boils and starts to turn lightly golden around the edges of pan. Stir in sesame seeds and reduce heat as low as possible to keep glaze warm during the dipping of the apple slices.

SINGAPORE □ The name Singapore—which means "Lion City" in Sanskrit—has been used for nearly one thousand years for this small island just off the southern tip of the Malay Peninsula in Southeast Asia. The name was probably given by mistake because the animals that used to roam the island were tigers, not lions.

A more accurate name was given to this island nation by Joseph Conrad, who called Singapore "the thoroughfare to the East." Although Singapore is one of the smallest countries in Asia, it is also one of the most prosperous, with a highly developed economy. The country has the sixth busiest port in the world, produces a wide range of manufactured products, and is a major international financial center.

SRI LANKA

1⅔ cups sugar
1½ cups water
1¼ cups semolina
3½ cups flaked coconut
¼ teaspoon ground cardamom
½ teaspoon rose flower water
½ teaspoon vanilla extract
¼ teaspoon ground cinnamon
2 or 3 drops green or red food
  coloring

Coconut Squares

These rich, chewy, and moist cake squares are especially good along with slices of your favorite fresh fruits.

Combine sugar and water in a heavy saucepan and cook over medium heat, stirring constantly, until sugar dissolves and mixture comes to a boil. Add semolina and continue cooking, stirring constantly, until mixture comes to a boil again; cook for 1 minute more.

2. Lower heat and mix in coconut, cardamom, rose flower water, vanilla, cinnamon, and food coloring. Continue to stir until mixture thickens.

3. Remove from heat and pour into a greased 9x13-inch baking dish and let cool. Cut into 2-inch squares.

Yield: approximately 2 dozen squares

SRI LANKA □ Located just off the southeastern tip of India, the nation of Ceylon in 1972 restored its ancient Sinhalese name of Sri Lanka, which means "the resplendent land."

The name is well chosen because Sri Lanka, the twenty-fourth largest island in the world, is an exceptionally beautiful country with rich tropical plant life, fine beaches washed by the Indian Ocean, colorful landscapes, and sparkling underwater flora and fauna.

In addition to all this natural splendor, Sri Lanka has been famous for over two thousand years for its fine tea, spices, and precious gemstones.

THAILAND

Coconut Cream Custard

1 cup cream of coconut
¾ cup granulated sugar
¾ cup packed brown sugar
4 eggs, beaten
1 tablespoon (one envelope, ¼ ounce) unflavored gelatin dissolved in 1 cup water

The unusual combination of coconut cream and brown sugar gives this custard dessert a unique taste that you will not get from any other pudding.

1. Combine cream of coconut, sugars, and eggs in a heavy pot. Cook over low heat, stirring constantly, until mixture comes to a boil and thickens.

2. Add dissolved gelatin and continue boiling, while stirring, for 1 minute more.

3. Spoon into individual custard cups and chill in the refrigerator.
Yield: 8 to 10 servings

THAILAND □ Bangkok, the capital of Thailand, sits on the banks of the Menam Chao Phraya River and is very much a city of water. Bangkok was founded in 1782 but it did not have its first road until nearly one hundred years later, relying instead on a system of canals.

Although the city has grown to be one of the leading cities in Asia, with modern office and apartment buildings, four hundred Buddhist temples, shopping centers, and a bustling nightlife, it retains some of its water roots. There are motorboat taxis, floating markets with sampan stores, and a still existing system of canals busy with boat traffic.

THE ORIENT

CHINA

1 cup sugar
6 egg yolks
1 cup finely chopped blanched
   almonds
½ cup bread crumbs
1 teaspoon almond extract
6 egg whites, stiffly beaten

Almond Cookies

This cookie gets its appeal from its delicious almond flavor and chewy cake-like texture.

1. Preheat oven to 350° F.
2. Combine sugar and egg yolks and beat until creamy. Add almonds, bread crumbs, and almond extract, mixing well. Fold in egg whites.
3. Pour batter into two 8-inch round cake pans that have been greased and lined with wax paper.
4. Bake at 350° F for about 35 minutes, until lightly browned. Let cool in pans and cut into wedge-shaped cookies.

Yield: approximately 2 dozen cookies

CHINA □ The Great Wall of China is the largest construction project on earth. It stretches as a defensive barrier over 1,500 miles across northern China with at least another 500 miles of branches and spurs. The Great Wall was begun in 400 B.C. and work continued on and off for two thousand years until it was completed.

Parts of the Great Wall have crumbled and been repaired, and sections of it in Mongolia have yet to be discovered and mapped.

Although the Great Wall was not completely successful in stopping invaders from coming into China, it is providing new benefits today. Scientists are studying how the Great Wall has been affected by earthquakes in order to develop ways to minimize the damage they cause.

JAPAN

2 cups hulled strawberries
1 cup boiling water
1½ cups sugar
3 tablespoons (three envelopes, ¼ ounce each) unflavored gelatin softened in ½ cup water
2 egg whites, stiffly beaten
Custard Sauce (recipe follows)

Strawberry Mold With Custard Sauce

The delicate Japanese touch is immediately seen in this light and pretty gelatin mold filled with strawberries. It is a cool and refreshing treat on a hot summer day.

1. Neatly arrange 1 cup of the strawberries in the bottom of a circular mold. Set aside.
2. Combine boiling water and 1¼ cups of the sugar in a saucepan. Stir in softened gelatin and place saucepan in cold water. Set aside.
3. Combine remaining ¼ cup sugar and egg whites. Stir into gelatin mixture and beat well. Pour slowly over strawberries in mold.
4. Chill in refrigerator for 15 to 20 minutes, until set.
5. Remove from mold and fill center with remaining 1 cup of strawberries. Serve with Custard Sauce.
Yield: 6 to 8 servings

CUSTARD SAUCE

2 egg yolks
1 tablespoon flour
¼ cup sugar
1 cup warm milk
½ teaspoon vanilla extract

1. Mix together egg yolks, flour, and sugar in a saucepan. Stir in milk while cooking over low heat and then remove from heat.
2. Mix in vanilla and chill in refrigerator.

JAPAN □ The Japanese Emperor traces his ancestry to the Yamato emperors who reigned over much of central Japan nearly two thousand years ago.

This long history of imperial rule makes the Japanese royal family the oldest monarchy in the world.

KOREA

1¼ cups honey
¼ cup wine
1¼ cups water
2 cups flour
2 tablespoons corn or sesame oil
Cooking oil

Honey Flower Cakes

These rich cookies, made with honey and wine, are served in Korea on special occasions with afternoon tea.

1. Combine ¼ cup of the honey, wine, and ¼ cup of the water in a saucepan and cook over low heat, stirring constantly, for 5 minutes. Remove from heat and let cool.
2. Combine wine mixture with flour and corn oil and knead for 3 minutes. Roll out dough to ¾-inch thickness. Cut into flower shapes with cookie cutter.
3. Mix together remaining cup of honey and cup of water in a heavy

saucepan and cook for 5 minutes over low heat. Remove from heat and let cool. Set aside.

4. Heat cooking oil until it is very hot, add flower-shaped pieces of dough, one at a time, and deep-fry in hot oil until cookies float to the top.

5. Remove cookies from the hot oil and immediately place them in honey and water mixture. Let stand for at least 24 to 48 hours. The longer the cookies soak, the more crunchy they become and the better they taste.

Yield: approximately 2 dozen cookies

KOREA □ In one of the more memorable episodes of the wonderful television series "M*A*S*H," Major Frank Burns, in his usual paranoia, becomes alarmed when he sees a Korean family bury what he believes to be a land mine.

The "mine" turns out to be nothing more harmful than a kimchi pot. Kimchi is the traditional Korean relish made from cabbages, cucumbers, radishes, and red peppers and is stored underground in clay jars for aging during the winter months. This relish is used with almost all Korean dishes and, in a way, Major Burns was right. The very strong taste and spiciness of kimchi can be a real shock to the unwary diner the first time it is eaten.

THE SOUTH PACIFIC

AUSTRALIA

3 egg whites, at room temperature
1½ cups sugar
2 teaspoons vanilla extract
1½ teaspoons vinegar
¼ cup boiling water
1 cup heavy cream, whipped
4 cups sliced fresh fruits (kiwi, strawberries, bananas, peaches, etc.)

Meringue and Fruit Torte

When you try this large meringue shell filled with whipped cream and colorful slices of fresh fruits you will know that there is more to Australia than just kangaroos, koalas, and boomerangs.

1. Heat oven to 450° F.
2. Combine egg whites, sugar, 1½ teaspoons of the vanilla, vinegar, and boiling water in a large bowl. Beat for about 12 minutes, scraping sides of bowl continuously, until stiff peaks form and mixture holds its shape.
3. On a cookie sheet covered with aluminum foil, shape mixture into a round shell 8 inches across with the center of the shell ½ inch thick and the outer edges 2½ inches high.
4. Place cookie sheet in oven, turn oven heat off, and leave in oven for 4 to 5 hours with the door closed.
5. Add remaining ½ teaspoon vanilla to whipped heavy cream and spoon into center of the meringue shell. Arrange fruit slices on top of whipped cream and meringue.
6. Cut into wedges and serve immediately.

Yield: 8 to 10 servings

AUSTRALIA □ "Waltzing Matilda," one of the most popular songs of Australia and a song that is so identified with the land down under, has nothing whatsoever to do with dancing or a woman named Matilda.

A "matilda" in Australian slang is a backpack and the song is about hiking along the back roads.

FIJI

Yam Balls with Coconut Cream Sauce

4 yams or sweet potatoes
Coconut Cream Sauce (recipe follows)

These pleasant and uncomplicated yam balls are a perfect match to the idyllic image of a pleasant and uncomplicated life on a South Seas island.

1. Preheat oven to 400° F.
2. Bake yams for about 1 hour, until soft. Grind yams, with skin on, into a paste. Shape into 1-inch balls and top with warm Coconut Cream Sauce.

Yield: 4 servings.

COCONUT CREAM SAUCE
2 cups sugar
2 cups cream of coconut

Melt sugar over low heat. Add cream of coconut very slowly and boil 2 to 3 minutes, until mixture becomes very thick.

FIJI □ Yaqona is a very popular drink in Fiji, made from the ground roots of the pepper plant.

Although Yaqona, which is also called Kava, is enjoyed informally among friends as a social drink served in a half of a coconut shell, with conversation and story telling, there is also the elaborately stylized Yaqona ceremony in which the host prepares the drink in front of the guest of honor and serves it with much ritual and correctness.

It is considered a special sign of respect and recognition to be the guest of honor at a Yaqona ceremony.

NEW ZEALAND

2 egg yolks, beaten
Dash salt
1 tablespoon cornstarch
½ teaspoon vanilla extract
1 cup scalded milk
2 tablespoons sugar
2 egg whites, stiffly beaten
1 cup heavy cream, whipped
*12 kiwi fruits, peeled and crushed
    into a pulp, or 1 cup canned kiwi
    fruit pulp*
2 kiwi fruits, peeled and sliced

Kiwi Fruit Crème

There are two kinds of kiwis in New Zealand: one is a small flightless bird related to the ostrich and the other is a small green fruit. You might not ever see the small bird but after serving this great dessert just once you and your family will start seeing this small green fruit over and over again.

1. Mix together egg yolks, salt, cornstarch, and vanilla. Gradually add milk. Heat over gently boiling water, stirring constantly, until mixture becomes thick. Remove from heat and stir in 1 tablespoon of the sugar. Set aside to cool.

2. Beat remaining 1 tablespoon of sugar into beaten egg whites. Fold egg whites into cooled custard. Gently fold in whipped cream and kiwi fruit pulp.

3. Spoon into individual serving dishes and chill in refrigerator for 2 to 3 hours. Top with slices of kiwi fruit.

Yield: 4 servings

NEW ZEALAND □ The people of New Zealand think of their isolated island nation—the closest neighbor, Australia, is over one thousand miles away—as a unique place that is "God's own country." According to them, after creating the rest of the world God wanted to make one special place for His own enjoyment and that place was New Zealand.

New Zealand is, indeed, special with no deadly snakes, no poisonous insects, and no dangerous wild animals. This freedom from outside interference and dangerous predators made some of the birds rather lazy, preferring to walk on the ground rather than flying. The result has been the disappearance of their wings through evolution.

The best known of these flightless birds is the kiwi, which has become the country's unofficial national emblem.

PAPUA NEW GUINEA

¼ cup cornstarch
2 cups milk
2 tablespoons sugar
Grated peel of half a lemon
1 teaspoon lemon extract
Jam

Blancmange

This white creamy pudding has a light lemony flavor and is topped off with your favorite jam.

1. Combine cornstarch with ½ cup of the milk, mixing together well. Set aside.

2. Pour remaining 1½ cups milk into a saucepan and cook over medium heat. Add sugar and grated lemon peel, stirring gently. As mixture just begins to boil, remove from heat and stir in cornstarch and milk mixture. Return to heat and bring to a boil; let boil for 3

minutes, stirring occasionally. Remove from heat and add lemon extract.

3. Pour pudding into a wet 1½ quart mold and place mold in a shallow pan filled with cold water until pudding sets.

4. Chill in refrigerator. Loosen around edges and turn into a serving dish.

5. Top with jam.

Yield: 4 to 6 servings

PAPUA NEW GUINEA □ Warm temperatures and abundant rainfall in Papua New Guinea make that country a lush tropical garden with an enormous variety of exotic flowers, including two thousand kinds of orchids and two hundred types of rhododendrons.

Many of these beautiful flowers can be seen in the Botanical Gardens on the campus of the University of Papua New Guinea near the capital city of Port Moresby.

INDEX

145